Praise for *It's Not What You're Thinking*

The tools and ideas in this book are so vital for all in health care now. From the wonderful description of Dr. van Pelt's professional journey to his role as an incredible innovator and improver to the tools and methods all can use to make care better, there is learning for all. I'd recommend that all students—whether medical, nursing, or therapists—and leaders can learn and employ the wonderful learnings for improving care.

—Maureen Bisognano
President Emerita and Senior Fellow, Institute for Healthcare Improvement (IHI)

There's no social goal more important than rooting out the systemic errors that are killing 250,000 patients a year in America. And there's no better guide than the eloquent Dr. Rick van Pelt, who experienced up-close a near-catastrophic mishap and has devoted his career to the life-saving transformation of the health-care system.

—Larry Tye
Director, Blue Cross of MA (BCBSMA) Foundation's Health Coverage Fellowship
New York Times Bestselling Author

Deeply driven by purpose, values, and the power of reflection on life, the medical profession, and the delivery of healthcare, Dr. Rick van Pelt turned a most confronting experience in the clinical practice of anesthesia into a life's work to find pathways and solutions that would help healthcare and thereby help humankind. Spanning recall on the most personal interactions that happen in the crucible of the doctor-patient relationship to the need for profound systemic change in how health systems and practitioners conduct their work, this volume connects it all and helps us make sense of the need for change. Moreover, he describes an innovative approach to implementing durable and impactful change in a large, complex healthcare setting. His work matters.

—S. Bruce Dowton, MD
Vice Chancellor, MacQuarie University, Sydney, Australia

In this courageous account, Dr. Rick van Pelt candidly explores the profound professional and personal challenges that follow a serious adverse event in the medical field. He reveals the often-hidden emotional toll of such experiences, while underscoring the critical value of compassionate peer support. His journey demonstrates how an empathetic network and the incorporation of peer support principles are essential for creating a safe, collaborative learning environment for problem solving and growth. Helen Keller wisely said, "Alone we can do so little; together we can do so much." This book beautifully illustrates that sentiment, showing how connection and understanding turn shared challenges into collective solutions. It is a powerful testament to the enduring impact of empathy and collaboration in the medical profession, offering hope and inspiration for practitioners at every level.

—Susan D. Scott, PhD, RN, CPPS, FAAN
Nurse, Scientist/Adjunct Associate Professor, University of Missouri Health Care

Rick van Pelt, M.D. is a healthcare hero, but more importantly, he is an instrument of healthcare change. Dr. van Pelt has earned his stripes in healthcare and has the scars to prove it. In his book, Rick outlines the steps for improvements. It won't be obvious. It won't be easy. But it needs to get done.

The delivery of healthcare in the United States continues to flounder despite incredible advances in diagnostics, medical treatments, and surgical interventions. This has become magnified with the introduction of universal healthcare, urgent care centers, emergency departments, clinics and hospitals are routinely overwhelmed with patients with the bedside providers bearing the burden and the blame of disjointed and fragmented care.

I have worked alongside Rick, delivering patient care. I have worked with Rick fixing problems with "quality improvement" steps. Just as easily as Rick can diagnosis disease, he easily identifies inefficiencies in care delivery. Rick recognizes that the solution is almost always "not what you think." He is able to see the long-term repairs required rather than adding a bandage. His successful methods are based on mitigating conflict and functional change. I advise those in healthcare delivery systems to read his book and implement his methods. You will be delivering better care.

—John Fanikos, BS, MBA
Director, Strategic Initiatives, North American Thrombosis Forum, Brookline, MA

Dr. van Pelt offers a refreshingly honest look at healthcare's challenges and presents an innovative approach to problem-solving. By integrating personal experiences with systemic analysis, he provides valuable insights for transforming healthcare from the inside out.

—Anthony Patterson
Associate Dean, Clinical Affairs and Strategy, CEO Emeritus, UAB Hospital

It's Not What You're Thinking is the right book at the right time as all leaders work to transform their organizations for current and future success. There's no way around conflict and differences, finding a way through it is what is essential. This book provides ways of thinking and ways of doing to achieve true collaboration.

—Christy H. Lemak, PhD
Professor and Chair Emerita, Dept. Health Services Administration, UAB School of Health Professions

Working alongside Dr. van Pelt and the clinical transformation office at UAB has been an inspiring journey of collaborative problem solving. Their innovative approach using the

3D prioritization and precision problem solving framework has led to meaningful, sustained change across departments. By fostering a culture of open communication and minimizing conflict, we've been able to improve patient care and operational efficiency in profound ways. It's been a privilege to be part of this transformative work.

—Kimberly Payne
Vice President, Clinical Operations, UAB Medicine/UAB Hospital

It's Not What You're Thinking is a must-read for anyone seeking to create lasting, high-impact change in their organization or personal endeavors. The book provides a powerful framework for understanding how to drive meaningful transformation while managing the inevitable challenges that come with it. I have personally worked closely with Dr. van Pelt to solve some long-standing inefficiencies that were driven by both culture and tradition. In utilizing strategies found in this book, we have been able to resolve disputes, turn conflict into a catalyst for innovation, and navigate complex situations resulting in change that has endured.

—Alison R. Garretson
Interim Vice President, Care Continuum and Care Transitions, UAB Medicine/UAB Hospital

Dr. Van Pelt has been key in transforming practice culture at UAB. His understanding of the integral role of systems, high performing collaborative teams, professionalism with associated peer support, and the implementation of principles of change management, has been the source of his success. His approach of sustained learning: to understand with humility and curiosity and to rethink and pivot with the powerful lessons articulated by Adam Grant. In the complex and ever-changing environment of health care, incentives and motivators are too often misaligned, leading to disenfranchisement of physicians and staff and ultimately burnout. Dr. Van Pelt's approach works to align the key psychological needs of self-determination and intrinsic motivation including competence, autonomy, and purpose as part of the transformative change within teams. The success of his work is important not only to the wellbeing of the providers but it's absolutely critical to the safety of the patients we take care of.

—Dan E. Berkowitz, MD
Professor and Chair, Department of Anesthesiology and Perioperative Medicine, UAB Medicine/UAB Hospital

Transformational change is difficult to achieve in a complex high volume, high acuity medical environment that involves multiple, intertwined patient care platforms. This became blatantly clear to me as a leader who had tried unsuccessfully to bring about effective, sustainable change to our practice in an effort to improve efficiency and quality outcomes measures for our trauma service. Dr. Van Pelt's process of maximal engagement of key stakeholders in an iterative and thoughtful approach deconstructed pressure points of conflict and created a practice redesign that resulted in remarkable improvements in key metrics that exceeded our expectations. Improved efficiencies in the care process have increased patient care capacity and eliminated diversion issues, allowing us to remain continuously available for our community in their time of need. It has also resulted in the best quality outcomes measures in the history of our trauma program. Building on this initial success, we have engaged Dr. Van Pelt in other patient care related restructuring processes with similar results. I am glad that Rick has decided to share his process so that others can likewise realize its benefits.

—Jeffrey D. Kerby, MD
Professor and Division Director, Trauma and Acute Care Surgery, UAB Medicine/UAB Hospital

Health care workers will recognize my experience as a physician: despite the dedication and skill of the staff, care delivery often remains fragmented, contentious, and overly complex. This environment can breed frustration and cynicism. However, I have transformed my perspective by learning from Dr. Van Pelt and embracing precision problem solving. This approach fosters an understanding of diverse viewpoints, clarifies core issues, and enables the development of impactful, sustainable solutions. As a result, teams emerge revitalized and motivated. Having successfully applied precision problem solving with numerous teams across various contexts, I wholeheartedly endorse its transformative potential!

—David McCollum, MD
Hospitalist UAB Hospital Medicine, Associate Principal, Clinical Transformation Office (CTO), UAB Medicine/UAB Hospital

Dr. van Pelt details his journey in healthcare from surgical internship to transformational problem solving in a way that challenges your assumptions about *why* we continue to face deficits in healthcare quality, safety, and efficiency. This book offers a unique paradigm for problem solving, based on systems principles and human nature, which can elevate our existing quality tools and forge a path for transformative changes in healthcare.

—Carlie Dobbins, MHA
Director of Operations, Clinical Transformation Office (CTO), UAB Medicine/UAB Hospital

As a healthcare leader who has spent years at the frontlines of patient care and organizational transformation, I can confidently say that the methodologies outlined in this book—3D prioritization and precision problem solving—aren't just theoretical frameworks, but practical tools that can drive real change in clinical environments. Rick's candid reflections in the chapter *"Another Day of Surgery: From Catastrophe to Catalyst,"* are incredibly inspiring. His openness not only humanizes the challenges we face as healthcare professionals but also shows how even the worst moments can spark innovation (and, let's be honest, a few sleepless nights).

I was a new nurse manager on a very busy medical-surgical unit when I first met Rick. My first thought? "Oh, great. Another project to manage." But that feeling faded fast as he demonstrated real support in developing a new process on our unit. Before I knew it, we had built an incredibly strong, cohesive leadership team across disciplines. Honestly, I'd never experienced that level of teamwork outside of direct patient care.

Now, let me tell you about the coffee. His team made having the best coffee on the unit a thing. Seriously? Coffee? We're talking about *hospital coffee*—how good could it possibly be? But somehow, it became a rallying point and my first experience with 3D thinking. And let me tell you, I've been using that approach ever since, across roles and teams. The methodology may start with something as small as coffee, but it turns into transformative leadership strategies that have long-lasting impact on patient care. This book is a must-read for any leader looking to inspire real, sustainable change (and maybe upgrade their caffeine game in the process).

—Toni Beam, MSN, RN, NE-BC
Nurse Wellness Manager, WE CARE Program, UAB Medicine/ UAB Hospital

It's Not What You're Thinking

Dr. Rick van Pelt

It's Not What You're Thinking

PRECISION PROBLEM SOLVING
WITH NO HYPOTHESIS

Advantage | Books

Published by Advantage Books, Charleston, South Carolina.
An imprint of Advantage Media.

ADVANTAGE is a registered trademark, and the Advantage colophon is a trademark of Advantage Media Group, Inc.

Printed in the United States of America.

10 9 8 7 6 5 4 3 2 1

ISBN: 978-1-64225-850-9 (Hardcover)
ISBN: 978-1-64225-849-3 (eBook)

Library of Congress Control Number: 2024923063

Cover design by David Taylor.
Layout design by Ruthie Wood.

This publication is designed to provide accurate and authoritative information in regard to the subject matter covered. It is sold with the understanding that the publisher is not engaged in rendering legal, accounting, or other professional services. If legal advice or other expert assistance is required, the services of a competent professional person should be sought.

Advantage Books is an imprint of Advantage Media Group. Advantage Media helps busy entrepreneurs, CEOs, and leaders write and publish a book to grow their business and become the authority in their field. Advantage authors comprise an exclusive community of industry professionals, idea-makers, and thought leaders. For more information go to **advantagemedia.com**.

To Linda. The power of your authentic outreach with "How are you doing?" was transformative. Thank you.

Contents

Acknowledgments

Life is about relationship, continuous learning, and action. The development of Precision Problem Solving is ongoing, and over the years I have had the opportunity and privilege to engage with many inspirational champions, teams, and organizations committed to transforming healthcare. To all of my fellow collaborative learners and change agents, thank you all for sharing the journey and for contributing to the growth and refinement of this methodology.

To my dearest colleagues and friends within our UAB Clinical Transformation Office, thank you for your commitment, innovative spirit, and boundless energy to bring PrecisionPS to functional life. The sustained impact you have created with our UAB Hospital teammates is a testament to the collective genius that becomes accessible when we create safe conditions for collaborative learning and prioritize our efforts in understanding and solving the functional problems that matter most to our frontline teams, patients, and families.

Thank you, Maria and family, for your unconditional support, encouragement, and patience throughout the nights and weekends of writing and rewriting the manuscript. A special thanks to Juliana for her book illustrations. I am so fortunate and grateful to be surrounded by such love.

My deepest gratitude to you, Karen, for your tireless assistance in developing, writing, and shaping this book. Your enthusiasm, creative insights, and talents as a writing coach and editor enabled us to move from an initially undefined book concept to one that we shaped into a story with a compelling message for transformation. I have learned a great deal over the two years we worked on this project and have a deeper understanding of the collaborative synergies that create conditions for continuous transformative change. Thank you, Karen. I could not have written this book without your guidance and support.

Introduction

This is not a how-to book. This is not a book about ideas. This is not a book trying to convince you of anything. This is not a quick and easy read.

Our healthcare system is in crisis despite all the advances we have achieved in modern healthcare and the dedicated care team members who work tirelessly to deliver the best patient care every day. Healthcare costs are skyrocketing; quality and patient safety remain formidable problems; capacity, access, and throughput barriers are daunting; and caregiver burnout is at an all-time high.

Our healthcare system is exceedingly complex, with intricacies and interconnections that are poorly understood. Conventional problem-solving approaches have achieved pockets of excellence, and sadly, our overall improvements have been marginal and unsustainable. The problems we are addressing today are largely the same as they were decades ago. For example, the Institute of Medicine's report *To Err Is Human,* published in 1999, estimated that up to 98,000 patients die each year due to medical errors.[1] More recent estimates from 2012

---

1   Institute of Medicine (US) Committee on Quality of Health Care in America, *To Err Is Human: Building a Safer Health System*, eds. L. T. Kohn, J. M. Corrigan, and M. S. Donaldson (Washington, DC: National Academies Press, 1999), PMID: 25077248.

estimate that number being closer to 250,000 deaths per year, putting medical error as the third leading cause of death after heart disease and cancer.[2]

Healthcare is in dire need of transformation. Our conventional problem-solving approaches push us to identify problems that we think are important and drive us to jump to ideal solutions based on what we think they should be. Our limited objective understanding of what is actually causing the problems and our subjective differences of opinion about cause and effect generate fragmentation and conflict, which ultimately produce suboptimal solutions and outcomes. Surely, there is another way to problem solve.

This book invites us to explore our current approach to problem solving objectively and enable our comprehensive understanding to define a new transformation paradigm. The approach to understanding a problem is more important than the problem itself. Transformation is possible when we understand the nature of conflict, the synergistic core principles of systems, participatory management, peer support, and the functional framework of Learning to Look, Looking to Understand, and Understanding to Act. We call this Precision Problem Solving.

This book has no shortcuts and no single most important chapter to read in isolation. As with solving a complex problem, our comprehensive understanding of the story reveals the embedded essence with which to act. Learning to Look is the foundation of transformative problem solving; everything develops from there. As you will see in the book's first section, Learning to Look can be an arduous and prolonged challenge.

---

2   M. A. Makary and M. Daniel, *Medical Error—the Third Leading Cause of Death in the US, BMJ* 353 (May 3, 2016): i2139, doi: 10.1136/bmj.i2139. PMID: 27143499.

So much of what we do and aspire to become is driven by our ingrained assumptions and expectations. We avoid some ambitions completely, and when we experience fortuitous course corrections on the paths we pursue, it is easy for us to attribute them to serendipity and to fall right back into our conventional routine of hurtling forward until we collide with the next barrier. Sometimes, it takes a profound adverse event to create insight into the transformative power of observing with no hypothesis.

This book is for the curious reader who is pulled to understanding and moving beyond the barriers to open inquiry. It's for the one who is open to exploring a functional methodology for compassionate problem solving together for sustained transformative change.

It's not what you're thinking.

SECTION I

Learning to Look

Chapter 1

Luck, Serendipity, and Precession

When you're surrounded by people who share the same set of assumptions as you, you start to think that's reality.

—EMILY LEVINE

I always wanted to be a pilot. My parents are from Europe, and traveling has been a constant in my life. The excitement and allure of global travel destinations, and especially the idea of flying myself to and from locations as a profession, only increased my passion for the science and technology of aviation, never mind the breathtaking freedom that comes from soaring thirty-five thousand feet above the hustle of daily life.

My father came from a Dutch family replete with sea captains and ship engineers, and my grandfather worked for KLM Royal Dutch Airlines. With this hereditary predisposition fueling my aspirations, my chosen path was unsurprising. I'd never wanted anything more. Yet, I didn't pursue this goal with the usual tenacity of my earlier years, probably because I didn't want an official confirmation of what I already knew and dreaded.

As a child, my parents and I had a hunch that I had inherited another family trait called color blindness—a vision deficit I knew would impede my ability to pass the required flight physical exam for pilot training. It was unbearable to think this physical hindrance could keep me from flying. To keep my dream alive, I played the denial game. But even as I tried to convince myself that I had normal color vision using self-created color tests, such as calling out the colors of cars as they passed, a nagging, sinking feeling persisted. I realized I would have to close the door on this ambition, as my father had with his dream of becoming a ship captain.

My grandparents were very practical, and my no-nonsense grandmother, knowing my father was completely color-blind as he strolled around in mismatched socks, set out to nip his unrealistic goal in the bud. The very instant the words "sea captain" left his mouth, she promptly took him to a doctor for an eye exam, which confirmed his color deficit, and that was the end of that. My father couldn't be a color-blind ship captain any more than I could be a color-blind airline pilot. Although he deeply empathized with my desire to be a pilot, he gently yet firmly encouraged me to expand my career horizons should aviation not work out.

Practicing medicine was another alluring career pathway for me, not just because my father and mother are physicians but also because I was a potential fifth-generation physician on my mother's side. I'd always been interested in medicine, but with that profession came an intense and competitive application process and training progression. I had always set very high expectations for myself academically and athletically, and even though I excelled in those areas, I had a strong aversion to the self-imposed pressure it created.

I couldn't imagine subjecting myself to that kind of stress for any profession, particularly when comparing it to an aviation career that I was passionate about and naively perceived as being much less competitive. When junior year arrived, I was actively considering aviation-focused colleges that were off the typical beaten path for my high school classmates. Focusing on aviation-centered colleges meant I wouldn't have to worry about entering the rat race of getting into an elite university to maximize my competitiveness for getting into medical school. But common sense prevailed with the realization that the likelihood of becoming a commercial pilot with my color deficit was slim to nonexistent.

Logic and tradition dictated that I park the aviation dream in the hangar and make medicine my career trajectory. So, in my senior year, I joined the college competition with my classmates and expanded my college search to include the requisite national rank and academic reputation. I was set on excluding nearby universities because I wanted a college experience far from home. This put Amherst College, located in my hometown, unquestionably off the radar, and not just due to its location. My mother also worked there as the Director of Student Health Services, and I couldn't imagine being on the same small campus with her, potentially bumping into her at inopportune moments. No need for parental surveillance, thank you very much! Amherst was an absolute no-go. Or so I thought.

Luck is the prepared mind at a serendipitous moment.

—MARK TWAIN

As luck would have it, I attended Amherst Regional High School with an upper classmate whose father was the Dean of Admissions at Amherst College. Upon hearing from our high school guidance counselors that her father would be happy to advise anyone on the college admissions process, I thought, why not? With my path still open, free college advice was an invitation I couldn't refuse. But I still had no intention of attending Amherst College. It didn't even cross my mind to show up for our scheduled session wearing anything other than my usual high school attire of jeans and a rugby shirt.

My conversation with the dean was surprisingly captivating, and by the end of our discussion, he concluded that I was "exactly the type of student Amherst was looking for." If I applied, he intimated that Amherst would accept me. Seriously? I left his office scratching my head at the serendipity of it all. I had no intentions when I walked into his office. None. Yet I was leaving with an incredible backup college, and suddenly the pressure of college acceptance had been lifted off my shoulders. I suddenly had the green light to push the envelope, so I began applying primarily to "stretch" universities, including Harvard and Swarthmore, and my now backup college, Amherst.

As the dean had suggested, I received my acceptance letter to Amherst shortly after applying, and a few weeks later, the Amherst football coach reached out to me with an invitation to spend a day on campus with some of their football players in the hope I may want to play for them. I had nothing to gain but also nothing to lose, so I accepted the invitation. By the end of that afternoon, I had made up my mind: I was going to Amherst!

The campus felt comfortably distinct from my high school "townie" experience, and an Amherst degree with completed premed requisites would give me a great shot at medical school. I was fired up. Even sharing a college campus with Mom seemed doable. Everything was set. I felt good about my new path, and it was clear now that all the mental stress I'd experienced prepping for college had been self-imposed. There had been no need to get sucked into the intense high school mindset of carefully constructing an exceptional application portfolio with advanced classes, high grade point averages, exceptional test scores, and a plethora of club activities. By taking classes and participating in activities that I enjoyed and excelled in, I unintentionally caught the favorable attention of college admissions officers at competitive schools. It was my first memorable experience with the phenomenon of precession.

Of course, all of this would have been a lot more significant had I been familiar with the term and concept. R. Buckminster, or "Bucky" Fuller, a renowned twentieth-century architect and innovator, defined the principle of precession, which describes the phenomenon of having purposeful activity emerge unintentionally beyond established goals. To illustrate precession, Bucky Fuller used his well-known analogy of the honeybee gathering nectar to make honey while inadvertently yet purposefully cross-pollinating plants as it buzzed from flower to flower.

In pursuing the defined objective, other important "side" activities took place, which supported and enhanced the defined objective: pollination maintains or increases the number of flowers for making honey. The sequence of events I'd perceived as luck had been precession at play: the rigidly defined trajectory for college admission and career progression we were all on was superseded by the high school activities I had innately done in the background. As much as I would have loved the effortless outcome of the application process to have signaled smooth sailing in the future, my lack of awareness of precession and continued self-competitiveness created fertile ground during my college years for their own trials and tribulations.

I began my first year at Amherst College in September 1982, and almost immediately, the self-imposed intensity of the next educational phase began, mostly because I was intent on combining premed course requirements with liberal arts course offerings while the academic window of opportunity was open. Many of my mother's family still lived in Germany, and I was eager to attend Tübingen University in Germany for my third year as an international exchange student. To make it happen, I'd have to compress the required premedical science classes into my first two years rather than the usual three.

As daunting as that felt, my unwavering resolve to study in Germany kept me pinned to my goal, and it had unintended consequences. I was struggling with the premed course load, and by the end of my second year, I had earned a couple of average science grades, notably in organic chemistry, which could affect my chances at med school acceptance. I was deeply frustrated, but since there was nothing I could do to change these results, I pressed on with my plans for an adventure in Germany.

There are downsides to everything; there are unintended consequences to everything.

—STEVE JOBS

I lived in Zaire, Africa, for three years with my family when I was ten to thirteen years old, which made for a youthful adventure and an early appreciation of social and healthcare inequities relative to the US. Although I experienced Zaire through innocent childhood eyes, the disparities left a lasting impression on me as an area of dire need and an opportunity to contribute. Because of my desire to serve the underserved and strengthen my medical school candidacy, I was set on getting international volunteer experience during college.

The summer after my sophomore year, I signed up with Amigos de las Americas. This organization deploys high school and college students to Latin and South American countries to assist with health and hygiene projects such as sanitation, eyeglass distribution, and immunizations. Amigos assigned me to a village near Acapulco, Mexico, to work on a latrine sanitation project with two high school students. I was excited about the adventure ahead, and although I felt uniquely prepared for the trip because of my experience in Africa, the mission took an immediate turn for the unexpected upon our arrival in Acapulco.

Amigos had neglected to tell us that the actual location of our remote village, Ojitos de Agua, was a six-hour bus ride from Acapulco high into the mountains. As our team triad boarded the local bus to Ojitos with local villagers, their chickens and goats as copassengers, a great unease swept over me. This was not going to be anything like my previous Zaire stint.

Our rural mountain village was home to approximately thirty families, and the three of us were matched with separate host families who lived in adobe single-bedroom homes. Being enveloped in extreme poverty was more than I'd expected, and I was humbled by our host families' kindness and gracious efforts to give us the best of everything they had. The mountain weather was much cooler than tropical Acapulco, and none of us had brought the right clothing for the cold night temperatures, leaving us to improvise how to dress in multiple layers of our summer clothing to stay warm.

The dilapidated cot I'd brought was much too low to the ground, and an unforeseen tear in its canvas cover worsened with every toss and turn I made to get comfortable. So, I had to come up with a specific bedtime routine. I felt like a gymnast on the parallel bars whenever I had to get on or off the cot. Once positioned, I had to remain perfectly still to prevent the damaged cot from collapsing further. It was no easy task to remain immobile, particularly with the added torment of a nightly invasion of bloodsucking "kissing" bugs that would climb up from the dirt floor, making their way into my layers of clothing, crawling and biting me up and down my body. It was a repetitive ordeal, one I could do little about if my cot was to last for the month, so I just had to let it be part of the experience.

Due to poor sanitation and water contamination, meals also quickly became a daily game of roulette. Any food that deviated from fried tortillas and eggs resulted in stomach upset and diarrhea. Pepto Bismol became a mainstay beverage, and on occasion, the village healer would attempt to cure my symptoms without much success.

To challenge us further, our construction supplies were delayed, impeding the volunteer work before it even started. Within the first day, I'd burned through the novel I'd brought with me, and with no diversions left, I quickly became antsy and irritable. But we found a way to forge ahead. Drawing on the memory I had of my father guiding and supporting local clinicians to set up their own healthcare clinics in Zaire, we began educating the villagers on the benefits of improved hygiene and encouraged them to take on digging the latrine pits.

Our goal was to inspire the villagers to take ownership of the work rather than imposing this initiative on them; we hoped that involving them in the construction would maximize villager engagement and sustain their hygiene practices. A group of willing villagers dug out their six-foot-deep latrine pits, which was no easy task in the dense, claylike soil, and when the supplies finally arrived two weeks into our stay, we were able to utilize the cement and rebar to make the latrine platforms. With the collaboration of the village, twenty-seven new latrines were constructed, and for the first time, almost every home had a private latrine.

The experience left me transformed, both physically and mentally. Physically, I'd lost twenty-five pounds because of the eating challenges. But more important was the wondrous and unique change within me. With very little diversion in those first two weeks in the quiet village setting, my restlessness morphed into a sense of calm and quiet as I began to assimilate with the villagers in their mountain habitat.

I had no choice but to focus on what was happening moment by moment. The acceptance of physical hardship and inescapable idleness by American standards became an unanticipated gift that helped me begin to embrace the peace that comes with slowing down, staying present, and actually paying attention to my surroundings. It was the beginning of seeing things through an inclusive lens and my first brush with being committed to serving without attachment to outcomes. I'd given my all to my team and the villagers and had accepted whatever outcome was achieved. Once again, a rigid objective had corresponding unintended peripheral benefits that I would never have expected. Precession at work.

I was barely home a week from Mexico when I took off again to start my third year studying in Tübingen, Germany. It was a brilliant opportunity for me to study at the same historic university where my mother had, to visit relatives, and to sample the cultural diversity of the European continent, breweries and all. I also successfully completed my medical college admission test (MCAT) requirement at a US military base in Germany and achieved a competitive score that I hoped would counterbalance my average chemistry course grades. My year abroad had exceeded my expectations in all respects, justifying the prior two-year premed course cramming, associated stress, and suboptimal impact on my grade point average. I had yet to experience the unintended consequences of my decisions.

Your value does not decrease based on someone's inability to see your worth.

—ANONYMOUS

I got back to Amherst in August 1985, one month before the start of my senior year, and began to organize the medical school application process. I set up a meeting with my premed advisor at Amherst College, who took one look at my grades, shook his head with dismay, and informed me that I was not a competitive medical school candidate. His advice? Don't bother applying.

Feeling beaten down and defeated, I went home, not having the foggiest notion of what to do next. I was living at home that year to save my parents some college expenses, and as I was stewing in distress, I found a brochure for a Caribbean medical school not so inconspicuously planted on my desk. Mom. She no doubt meant well, but this managed to deflate my spirits even more. My father was not so easily dissuaded. He worked at UMass Health Services in Amherst and was an associate faculty member at UMass Medical School (UMMS). He felt strongly that UMMS was well recognized for its medical training and affordability and made the outrageous suggestion that I apply for Early Decision. Crazy. Just plain crazy. Especially given my academic standing and the lack of confidence my premed advisor had just conveyed. Since Early Decision meant I could apply to only that school, this would set me back months on applications to other schools if I were rejected. But I had put a lot of resolve, time, and effort to get this far, and my father's optimistic confidence rekindled my determination. Blinking hell, I was going for it!

I applied for Early Decision to UMMS, and two weeks later, I was thrilled to receive a letter of invitation to interview. Although the little voice in my head wondered if this was a courtesy invite due to my father's UMass affiliation, it wouldn't hold me back during the interview. In full transparency, I addressed my perceived premed academic shortfall directly with my medical school interviewers and was pleasantly surprised by the lack of interest and concern that they had for "a few average grades."

One of my interviewers seemed particularly taken by the diversity of my college course load and extracurricular activities and sent me on my way, saying, "I am going to call you curious." I left the interview cautiously optimistic, and a week later, I received my formal letter of acceptance into the UMass Medical School class of 1990. Joy and relief flooded me. This locked door had unexpectedly opened when I'd let go of assumptions and expectations and acted. Every activity peripheral to my hardcore pursuit of meeting the rigorous premed requirements was the main determinant for acceptance. Precession again. With the early acceptance to med school, the pressure of applying had been lifted less than a month into my senior year. I relished the remainder of my final college year as I readied myself for the demanding medical training ahead of me. I could not foresee the disaffection that would become a regular part of my daily life.

Chapter 2

Trust No One: Entering the Quality Chasm

A frog dropped into hot water will immediately jump out; a frog dropped into temperate water that is gradually heated will not.

—THE BOILING FROG FABLE

It felt great to finally be in medical school with my ninety-nine classmates. While we did have some exposure to direct clinical care as part of our didactic curriculum during the first two years, I couldn't wait to begin full-time third-year training in the actual patient care settings. But as the third-year clinical rotations approached, wariness began to creep in with the sobering awareness that I would be assuming care responsibilities that would directly impact patient lives. The medical oath, "First do no harm," was starting to have real meaning. The responsibility for providing high-quality and safe patient care seemed untenable with the concurrent need to master the vast content, complexities, and uncertainties in diagnosing and treating clinical disease. The myriad of systems-related quality and safety issues would further challenge our ability to master patient care delivery.

Descending into the healthcare quality chasm was gradual and obscure. Similar to how military boot camp is portrayed, medical training was full of stories of the looming hardships and endurance tests that would be part of the progression. Long work hours, night calls, hierarchical roles and responsibilities, intimidating and demanding physician attendings, and punitive intolerance of low performance and mistakes morphed quickly from lore to reality. As stomach-churning as this high-stress environment became, we viewed it as another challenge to overcome, one that would demonstrate that we had the fortitude to become physicians and that we had "the right stuff."

We were part of the care team now and expected to put in an enormous number of hours, largely mirroring the interns and residents, whose expected practice was to remain in the hospital until the work was done. This often resulted in work obligations exceeding one hundred hours per week. Our repetitive and inefficient care activities demanded the intense effort of every team member, and to be absent for any time meant considerable hardship for the remaining group. This reinforced our cultural norm of mandatory team presence, barring deathly illness and extreme duress. The fatigue, care demands, and commitment to our patients created an extraordinarily strong team bond, an esprit de corps, which became an essential survival mechanism and energy source to help us endure the training.

The ubiquitous challenge of providing high-quality and safe patient care in a dysfunctional care setting with workarounds became our daily struggle on every clinical rotation. Tasks and processes such as ordering labs, scheduling patients for x-rays, or requesting subspecialty consults were often misaligned with our primary team efforts to move patients' care along efficiently. High-impact patient safety events would often expose us to the inherent risks associated with poorly designed complex care processes and the resulting culture of blame and shame. This was made poignantly evident to me during my surgical rotation by a patient who had been scheduled to have both knees replaced sequentially over weeks, starting with the left knee.

We completed routine preoperative preparation with the patient, and it wasn't until the orthopedic team was well into the operation, having made the incision and prepared the knee joint for the replacement parts, that the team realized they were operating on the wrong knee. Although the reasons for the wrong-site surgery were unclear, finger-pointing immediately ensued to assign blame for the error. Regardless of the actual cause, we all knew that the attending surgeon would be soundly reprimanded at the next departmental morbidity and mortality conference.

The only reason real harm was averted was because both knees had been scheduled for replacement. Otherwise, this error would have had catastrophic consequences for the hospital and, more importantly, the patient. But to watch everyone's immediate response of distancing themselves from the event and the attending surgeon was a sobering experience, a deeply disturbing situation I would later experience when I landed at the sharp end of a catastrophic patient safety event. It was a well-practiced blame game, virtually guaranteeing that wrong-site surgery would inadvertently happen again since no one was looking for and addressing the actual cause of the error.

Plans are nothing; planning is everything.

—DWIGHT EISENHOWER

When I started medical school, I had aspired to become a pediatric surgeon. Fast-forward a couple of years, and already the long training hours, lack of quality personal life, and thought of three additional fellowship years after a five-year general surgery residency made me realize it wouldn't be a good fit. I was still hell-bent on becoming a surgeon, though, and it was while I was doing a head and neck (ENT) surgery rotation at the Mass Eye and Ear Infirmary (MEEI) in Boston with Dr. William Montgomery, fondly known as Monty, that I realized that ENT was the specialty for me. ENT dealt with a complex anatomy that few clinicians understood, which had great niche appeal.

The work-life balance I sought was evident in the dedication and enjoyment of the work among the residents and attending physicians alike. They loved what they did, and I was particularly taken by Monty's ability to remain truly humble despite his clinical brilliance and international recognition as one of ENT's founding fathers. He appeared to have no interest whatsoever in recognition or accolades, remaining ever inquisitive and focused on doing his best for patients. He loved to teach and was always looking to innovate. I had found my specialty and my mentor.

My knack for dogged focus when pursuing defined objectives led me to make the foolish move of only applying to select ENT programs. I was well aware of the extreme competitiveness for scarce ENT residency spots nationally, but I remained irrationally obstinate, even when strong indicators during the application process suggested that I would flame out; I had only received three interview requests where the norm for strong candidates was ten. Denial is a powerful blinder, and I was shocked when I didn't match. I hadn't considered a backup residency plan since I had no interest in anything else and found myself at a major impasse.

But I refused to be derailed and had to act fast. UMMS did not have an ENT residency program, and it was clear I would have to optimize next year's reapplication by securing a research position at a health system with an ENT program or a recognized freestanding research institution. I considered a list of potential research institutes, and the National Institutes of Health (NIH) popped out as a logical target. I was naive to research and had no contacts at NIH, so I made a Hail Mary cold call to the main NIH phone number. I was clearly throwing the operator a curveball as she tried to make sense of my situation and ambiguous research interest. But somehow it clicked for her, and she decidedly connected me to the National Institute for Deafness and other Communication Disorders (NIDCD).

The next thing I knew, I was speaking to one of the senior institute directors, who was leading a multiprofessional team on research in speech and voice disorders. Not only was the research ENT-related, but her team included a board-certified ENT surgeon and ENT residents on research rotation from Georgetown University. She had been looking for a research fellow, and fitting the bill, I was immediately offered the position of Intramural Research Training Award (IRTA) fellow. Precession had once again created an alternative path forward. But again, I had yet to be introduced to Bucky in my travels, so the precession that brought me here was still lost on me. Instead, I sat stunned and thrilled by what I still considered incredible luck. Whatever was at play behind the scenes, the road to ENT was alive, and I would spend the next year as an IRTA fellow at NIDCD in Bethesda studying speech and voice disorders.

Embrace the suck.

—USMC

As I had hoped, my year of research at NIDCD was a productive change from medical school and set me up as a highly competitive candidate for ENT residency. I matched at Mass Eye and Ear and kicked off my surgical training in July 1991 as a general surgery intern at the New England Deaconess Hospital (NEDH) in Boston. My first rotation began at a VA hospital in New Hampshire. It was an immediate reentry into the extreme workload, care inefficiencies, and quality and safety risks I'd blocked out while at NIH. At our first team briefing, our chief resident gave us the prime directive for patient care: *trust no one.* With the known pervasive lack of systems reliability in care delivery, I was responsible for ensuring everything that needed to get done was accomplished, even if that meant doing the most basic logistical tasks myself.

Before the other intern and I could orient to our newly acquired patient service, the hospital administration instructed us to complete over fifty patient discharge summaries that the preceding surgical team had left in their wake. We knew nothing about these patients, but given no alternative, we managed to complete the discharge summaries in short order. This was our introduction to proficient maneuvering through endless care challenges by developing work-around solutions to process inefficiencies.

"Trust no one" became the motto, and as my chief had intimated, I quickly found the only way to ensure all the daily tasks were completed was to do them myself. Tasks that should never have landed on my plate, such as drawing morning and evening labs on my twenty-five to thirty patients, became common when all the hospital phlebotomists responsible for drawing daily labs on patients called in sick. There were also special occasions, such as when the Joint Commission was doing a weeklong hospital accreditation visit. This was when I became proficient at doing blood sugar testing for my diabetic patients because hospital administration had confiscated all the bedside glucometers, which would not have passed inspection.

The commonly applied "See One, Do One, Teach One" model gave me on-the-job expertise in placing invasive cardiac monitors with little supervision. Our senior residents were intent on doing as many major surgeries as they could because of the autonomy that the VA system afforded them, and "someone" (me and my fellow intern, as it turned out) became responsible for getting our critically ill ICU patients ready for the operating room. Thank goodness for the critical care nurses who supported us.

The ten-week VA surgical rotation at the front end of the internship set me up for success in all the following rotations. In addition to assimilating the workaround mindset for getting the job done, I had also become adept at compartmentalizing my life into daily bite-size increments rather than thinking about the internship length in its entirety. As unpleasant as it remained, I had learned how to survive through fragmentation and emotional suppression, trusting no one but myself.

There would be plenty of additional endurance challenges that year, such as our ten-week Children's Hospital rotation, where we were on call five out of seven nights per week and spent over 150 hours in the hospital.

Due to the pervasive culture of practice autonomy and care variation, there would be ongoing exposure to the endemic tolerance of quality and patient safety lapses in care delivery. There would be unsettling lapses in surgical training, such as the introduction of laparoscopic gallbladder surgery, where inadequately trained community surgeons would inadvertently harm patients with procedural missteps, resulting in irreparable liver injury that put these otherwise healthy patients into catastrophic liver failure. These patients would be transferred to NEDH for liver transplantation as their only chance of survival. We were trying to deliver the best patient care possible in a care environment set up for failure. Vigilance was at the core of what we did. We kept our heads down, pressed on, and trusted no one.

An unanticipated reprieve from this snafu was when I was assigned to a couple of anesthesia rotations, which created envy and considerable discontent among my surgical teammates as an unwarranted leave of absence from the internship infantry. Since I was going into ENT, I presumed that the program directors had wanted me to have additional experience in airway management. I had been so intent on becoming a surgeon in medical school that anesthesiology had never even remotely surfaced as an interest or need for exposure, and I was surprised to discover how much I enjoyed it.

Providing high-acuity care using multiple technical interventions on very sick patient populations appealed to me. The anesthesia team was confident, disciplined, and very process-oriented, which stood out in stark contrast to the months of workaround care I had perfected during the other rotations. More importantly, the anesthesia residents always seemed to be doing meaningful work and enjoying all aspects of their responsibilities. Work-life balance seemed to be embedded in the anesthesia safety culture, and when the work was done at the end of the day, we went home with no loose ends, ready for new challenges the next day. The rotations gave me pause in thinking about my decision to enter ENT. Still, having invested so much effort into securing a residency, I concluded that deviating at this point would be sacrilege. I needed to stick with the game plan. Although internship had blunted the allure, there had to be a good reason I had chosen ENT.

The anesthesia rotations were transient blips of relief in the greater context of internship. It was an arduous, long journey, and for all the self-imposed survival tactics that I had learned to insulate myself with, were it not for the resident camaraderie that we established and depended on to get through each day, I'm not sure many of us would have tolerated the training conditions. But we had to play to stay, and the incentive to keep going was the unspoken promise that, eventually, things would get better. It was a rite of passage, a game of delayed gratification. I would take one day at a time for a year, and then my internship would be over. Everything would be better as a resident. Right?

Not so fast. By the time my internship ended on June 30, 1992, I realized just how naive my thinking had been.

Chapter 3

Delayed Gratification and
the Rite of Passage

The thing we call failure is not the falling down, but the staying down.

—MARY PICKFORD

On July 1, 1992, I reported to the Mass Eye and Ear Infirmary as one of five new ENT residents. In under twenty-four hours, I had miraculously transformed from menial general surgery intern into ENT resident, responsible and instantly capable of caring for patients with ENT ailments in the MEEI emergency room. While senior resident coverage was always available as a backup from remote locations elsewhere in the hospital, it was largely our charge as first years to learn how to manage patients with limited supervision. See one, do one, teach one. I was again part of an excellent resident team and privileged to work with talented and accomplished attending faculty. Dr. Janfaza, affectionately known as Dr. J., was the dedicated attending who guided and shepherded the first-year residents as we rapidly established our clinical acumen in our new specialty.

Despite finally having made it to what I had envisioned as my clinical career calling, there was a constant palpable tension in the residency program that was difficult to pinpoint. There had been resident attrition in the previous two years, which was virtually unheard of in highly competitive and limited-capacity ENT residency programs, particularly this one with its international reputation for excellence. It did not take long for me to realize that perhaps I had made a mistake. I couldn't escape the progressive sense of discontent, alienation, and striking absence of team cohesion and camaraderie.

There was also a persistent aura of comparative scrutiny for worthiness to be part of the MEEI residency program, a perceived need to demonstrate that I belonged. To make matters worse, the first year of residency was largely nonoperative, and we spent most of our days covering either the ER or our resident outpatient clinics. While the training objective made intuitive sense—getting in-depth exposure to outpatient ENT diagnosis and care—the volume of patients we would evaluate, upwards of thirty-two patients daily, pushed me toward burnout. I was at the beginning of my ENT training and already beginning to resent my patients. The interesting patients we diagnosed would immediately be handed off to the senior residents for further evaluation and potential surgery.

I reassured myself that it had to get better next year as I endured this schedule and pace those first nine months before starting my three-month rotation covering ENT services at the Brigham and Women's Hospital (BWH) and the Beth Israel Hospital. We were a two-resident team, a senior resident and me, and on call every other night and weekend for the twelve-week rotation. While this was a welcome reprieve from the Mass Eye and Ear ER and clinic, I was again in constant fatigue and distress as I managed most of the non-surgical ENT patient care while the senior resident operated. I'd lost all anticipation for a better next year, and it was too far away to matter. Burnout had set in. I was exhausted, unhappy, and trapped. Something had to change radically.

Experience is not what happens to you, it's what you do with what happens to you.

—ALDOUS HUXLEY

I completed my pre-rounding on April 13, 1993, and met up with my senior resident to review our patient list and care plan. Before starting our workday, he invited me along to have breakfast with one of his friends, a BWH anesthesia resident. I didn't have time or energy for this distraction but grudgingly agreed and dragged myself to the cafeteria with him. It was a beautiful spring morning, and I sat with them at the breakfast table in the sunshine while half listening to the anesthesia resident as he happily shared his postcall plan for the day—attending the Red Sox home opener at Fenway Park.

I could only scowl at him as I struggled to wrap my head around the notion of leaving the hospital to see a baseball game, like a real person with a real life. Getting out early for something fun and refreshing was a stark contrast to my busy postcall obligations that lasted well into the evening. I continued to glare, resenting my circumstances, when the anesthesia resident suddenly turned to me and somewhat jokingly said, "It's never too late to change." His unexpected comment struck me like a lightning bolt. I was thunderstruck and could only stare at him, stunned as his proposition sunk in. What seemed so obvious to him was suddenly so palpable to me. I had to switch out of ENT.

I was locked in again and wasted no time. While my senior resident went to the OR for the day, I made my way down to the BWH Department of Anesthesia office to inquire about opportunities for getting a residency position in their program. The department administrative assistant smirked with bemusement and reminded me that the residency match had already taken place the prior month. There was no available spot. But she didn't let me leave empty-handed, as she offered me an application form and suggested I find a few faculty members who could write letters of recommendation for me.

She promised to file them for potential future consideration. It was a toe in the door. Unfortunately, my only anesthesia experience was during my internship at the Deaconess across the street from the Brigham. I was undeterred, used to long shots, and promptly walked over to their Chief of Anesthesia's office, who happened to be between OR cases. He hadn't seen me in more than a year, and I was a surgical intern at that time, so he barely recognized me. I explained my interest in looking at the BWH anesthesia residency program and my need to be discreet. He skeptically offered to look through some of the performance evaluations they collected as part of the anesthesia training to see what he could do.

I walked back to BWH to catch up on my clinical duties with a sense of calm that I had not felt for quite some time. I had reestablished a clear direction and had done all I could under the current circumstances. The ball was in their court, and what happened next was out of my control. Things would play out the way they were supposed to.

The following day, I was contacted by the BWH anesthesia department's administrative assistant. To my great surprise, she informed me that the chairman was interested in setting up an interview and asked whether I could be available the following afternoon. What had just happened? Of course, I was available!

The next afternoon, the chairman and several other senior BWH anesthesia faculty interviewed me about my interest in anesthesia. They usually held a few residency spots open for qualified transfer candidates and asked if I could start that July if offered a position.

It was a perfect setup for me. I was committed to finishing the ENT training year through June so as not to disrupt or burden my resident colleagues with additional coverage responsibilities. The transition would be seamless. The next morning, I received the formal offer to become a BWH anesthesia resident. The chairman knew this was a big decision and suggested I take the weekend to think it over and respond back on Monday.

My excitement for this pivotal opportunity to realign my career trajectory was hampered only by the concern that I would be letting down people who had championed my successful acceptance into MEEI, especially my mentor, Monty. I had never considered myself a quitter, and enveloped in a surgical culture where long hours and hardship were the accepted norm to achieving clinical excellence, I felt a bit like a failure.

As I sat in this uncomfortable state, it dawned on me that my well-being rather than the opinions of others about my decision was what really mattered. Sure, I might leave a bad mark on the MEEI ENT program, and my departure would create a resident gap, but I had never fully felt a part of the program anyway—the current program culture made sure of that. This disconnect also helped me realize I was not as important to the program as I might have once assumed, and I would easily be replaced. Anesthesia was another opened door beckoning me to walk through. It was the right thing to do, and for the first time since starting my internship, I felt like I was regaining my ability to chart my own course. Without hesitation, I accepted the BWH residency position and gave Mass Eye and Ear my three-month notice.

The electric light did not come from the continuous improvement of candles.

—OREN HARARI

It was a refreshing change when I started my anesthesia residency in July 1993. Although this was the third consecutive year at the bottom of the training totem pole, the strong team-oriented training environment at BWH and the immediate emphasis on clinical OR anesthesia practice made the transition easy and meaningful. The three years of anesthesia residency progressed very quickly. I was finally on track in a specialty that I had never seriously considered because of my myopic drive to become a surgeon.

The anesthesia track met my clinical care expectations, I enjoyed coming to work every day, and the work-life balance felt optimal. This change, however, did not eliminate the underlying challenges within the care environment. In contrast to the performance, quality, and safety issues that I had dealt with during my years of surgical training, which seemed more intimate to direct patient care, the challenges that emerged during anesthesia training were much more centered on hospital operations.

Insurers created new coverage models that imposed additional requirements and restrictions on care delivery. Administrative activities that had been managed in the background and largely avoided by clinicians were now having direct and visible clinical impact. For example, shortly after I began my first anesthesia residency year, we were informed that preoperative hospitalization to prepare patients for scheduled surgery would become same-day admissions (SDA); surgical patients would now have to arrive ready for surgery on their scheduled OR day, with things like labs, x-rays, specialty consults, and paperwork completed beforehand in outpatient clinics. How was this supposed to work?

I was dumbfounded by how little operational planning and preparation had gone into this transition. Without a structured implementation process, all clinicians impacted by the change, including surgeons, anesthesiologists, nurses, and perioperative staff, resorted to new workarounds to adapt. Things that hadn't been completed beforehand were now done immediately prior to the surgery, which often caused significant delays. We were trading one inefficiency for another one. Thank goodness we were all accustomed to navigating systems dysfunction.

In another instance, the hospital administration hired a consulting firm to reduce costs and improve OR patient throughput. Without engaging perioperative faculty and staff, the clinicians doing the work, they decided to regulate access and distribution of surgical scrub attire using automated dispensing machines in place of the usual manual exchange process. Though conceptually compelling, the consultants had not considered the importance of matching availability of inventory scrub sizes with actual need, which resulted in a common shortage of correct sizes. One morning, in protest to the flawed implementation, one of the anesthesia attendings known for his exaggerated antics came into the OR wearing only a scrub top and underwear; the bottoms dispensed to him had been too small, and although this was not a very effective solution, the message was clear: faculty and staff delivering direct clinical care at the front line needed to be actively involved in creating sustainable solutions.

With all these dysfunctional changes at play, frustration and job dissatisfaction among faculty and nursing staff were at an all-time high. Without coordinated improvement plans, the added pressure from misaligned efforts to increase surgical volume and throughput efficiency exacerbated tensions within and across care teams. In a blame-oriented culture of quality and safety, the stressed work environment not uncommonly created flares of staff acrimony. As I had personally experienced during my ENT year, it was distressing to hear my attendings lament a growing feeling of compassion fatigue, the erosion of upholding the innate commitment to exceptional patient care and service, within a setting that constantly seemed to be derailing those objectives.

Despite these challenges, I remained committed to clinical care. I opted to extend my anesthesia training at BWH with a one-year fellowship in regional anesthesia, mastering the art and science of peripheral and central nerve blocks. About halfway through my fellowship, I recognized that as much as I enjoyed the practice of anesthesia, I was not going to survive as a clinician unless I understood the business side of healthcare that was so staunchly impacting clinical care. I wanted to take an active role in improving the care environment so that I wouldn't end up as a disempowered attending on the receiving end of misaligned directives from on high. I decided to explore options for getting an MBA.

A former anesthesia attending of mine had gotten an MBA and raved about his education at Harvard Business School (HBS). He shared that a collaborative effort was underway between HBS and Harvard Medical School (HMS) to create a joint degree program to develop physician leaders. Although the program had not been established, he encouraged me to apply as an HMS resident. His guidance inspired me, and my subsequent review of their case-based curriculum and a program option that would allow me to complete the MBA in sixteen months rather than the usual two years sealed my decision to apply only to HBS. Once again, I was putting myself in a high-stakes game of all or nothing; I was either going to HBS or I was not getting an MBA. As good fortune would have it, I was accepted into the HBS class of 1999 a few months after submitting my application.

Do the best you can until you know better. Then when you know better, do better.

—MAYA ANGELOU

I finished my regional anesthesia fellowship in June 1997 and remained on staff at BWH as an attending until January 1998, when I began my MBA degree as a full-time student. It was a considerable lifestyle adjustment for me, my wife, and my two young kids. Knowing I would be immersed in prohibitively time-consuming academics and team-based work assignments, we decided to sell our house and move into student-family housing on the HBS campus.

Despite the drastic downsizing of accommodation, it was a smart decision. My time at HBS was simultaneously one of my life's most rigorous and transformative educational periods. All my prior professional training, academic and practical, had centered on clinical sciences. For the first time, I immersed myself in business-related disciplines, including accounting, finance, operations management, negotiation, and organizational behavior. While most of my HBS classmates had worked in the business domain and were able to apply their business backgrounds to the exclusively case-based teaching approach, I found myself having to concurrently study textbook material to understand and apply these new concepts to the actual case studies being taught. This resulted in long hours of study and class, which became a study-sleep routine with family mealtime intermissions for the duration of the program.

As demanding as the academic workload was, I had an incredible time of discovery and appreciation for this entirely new field of business leadership. Much of the HBS curriculum was nonhealthcare focused. I was amazed by the similarities of problems that other industries faced relative to healthcare as well as the solutions that had been developed that could be adapted to healthcare. It became evident that healthcare had insulated itself from other industries and that we were far behind in many approaches being applied to improve quality, safety, and performance issues. During my second year, the course Managing Innovation, taught by Professors Clay Christensen and Gary Pisano, emerged as the lynchpin that validated my MBA pursuit.

I was captivated by the concept of disruptive innovation and the relevance that this had to healthcare, where innovative technologies were constantly being introduced haphazardly. I began to see an improvement approach I could bring back to healthcare to create strategic, relevant, and sustainable change. If I could find a role that enabled me to split my time between clinical anesthesia and leading performance improvement, I would be set up for a satisfying and fulfilling career.

I graduated from HBS in June 1999 and returned to the Brigham and Women's Hospital with a hybrid position that divided my time between clinical anesthesia and serving as the hospital's administrative Deland fellow. I had been very fortunate once again to have an unexpected pivotal contact with the BWH CEO at the time who, recognizing my interest in integrating clinical and administrative leadership around performance and quality improvement, had suggested that I take the fellowship role as a means of getting full access and opportunity to work with hospital C-suite leadership. To accommodate me, he had been willing to customize the fellowship to meet my administrative needs as a clinician, the opposite of the fellowship's stated intent of providing the reverse for administrators seeking clinical experience. I was poised to reenter healthcare as a clinician and a hospital performance improvement expert.

After nine years of postgraduate training, I was finally at a point where I felt prepared and excited to enter the workforce as a qualified healthcare professional. I had a great clinical position as an attending anesthesiologist, and I would be building my administrative expertise in performance, quality, and safety improvement as the Deland fellow. I had faced multiple challenges and trodden a winding path defined by dogged persistence and multiple abrupt course corrections that had fortuitously emerged. Somehow, precession had recalibrated my compass at pivotal waypoints despite my strong and frequently misguided sense of direction. Still, if I had known that those same waypoints would also lead me to a catastrophic and life-changing event, I might not have felt so lucky.

Chapter 4

Another Day of Surgery: From Catastrophe to Catalyst

You may not control all the events that happen to you, but you can decide not to be reduced by them.

—MAYA ANGELOU

On November 18, 1999, I was assigned to work with a foot and ankle surgeon in the OR's orthopedic pod. We were halfway through the day when I was called to the preoperative holding area to get our next patient ready. She was an otherwise healthy thirty-seven-year-old, a mother of three, who had a history of congenital clubfeet. She'd had multiple surgeries, was a frequent flyer within the health system, and was now coming for a definitive right ankle replacement after multiple prior corrective surgeries.

As a seasoned patient, she knew what she wanted and, more importantly, what she didn't want. In this case, she didn't want regional anesthesia. As a regional anesthesiologist and as part of a service that prided itself on delivering exceptional regional anesthetic care, I knew that she would benefit from having a combined general anesthetic with a regional nerve block for good postoperative pain control. I talked with her about her regional anesthesia concerns and discovered her prior experiences had been related to ineffective or unpleasant experiences with spinal and epidural anesthesia.

We discussed the advantages of using regional anesthetics for this type of procedure, mainly because it was a big surgery and ideal for the type of nerve block we commonly used, known as a popliteal fossa block. I assured her that I'd successfully completed many of these blocks in the past. She reluctantly agreed to proceed with the placement of this block behind the knee and to combine this with a general anesthetic. We also decided that if she became uncomfortable with how we were progressing during the placement of the block, we would revert to conventional postoperative pain control.

We positioned the patient on her stomach and followed the standard of care at the time. Using an electrical nerve stimulator approach, a type of electrical homing signal, we identified the targeted nerves and proceeded to incrementally inject the long-acting local anesthetic bupivacaine, making sure that she was not experiencing any signs or symptoms that would suggest improper placement. The patient tolerated the injection without discomfort or complaints, and we were happy with the result. As we were getting ready to take her into the operating room, she suddenly became very disoriented and agitated. Before we could react, her symptoms rapidly progressed to a grand mal or total body seizure. It was obvious she'd received at least a portion of the injection into her circulation, and I immediately called for help. I was fortunate to have a good team of experts available, and we quickly assembled around the patient as her condition deteriorated into cardiac arrest.

We proceeded with the typical interventions associated with cardiac resuscitation, but all had very little effect. Although we worked together quickly and efficiently, part of me observed the moment in stunned disbelief, desperately wanting even a few seconds' pause to grasp what had happened. What had I done wrong? But there was no time to process. We followed the OR director as he managed the code, and about ten minutes into the attempted resuscitation, we realized we needed to escalate the intervention to save her.

The only way to explain the next sequence of events was again one of serendipity, because everything that needed to be there was in place: there was an open cardiac operating room across the hall complete with surgical instruments laid out, a gowned and gloved scrub nurse, a circulator nurse, a primed bypass machine, a perfusionist, and even a cardiac surgical team that was waiting in the hallway for another patient to come down from the cardiac intensive care unit. We crashed across the hallway into that room, and within thirty minutes from the onset of the code, the patient was on the operating room table with her chest opened via a midline sternotomy and connected to the bypass machine. With the bypass machine started, we watched the EKG monitor with bated breath for any return of cardiac function. It was the longest minute of my life, but her rhythm gradually returned. Over the next hour and a half, we were able to successfully wean the patient off the bypass machine, close her chest, and prepare to move her to the cardiac intensive care unit. She was no longer an orthopedic patient but a recovering cardiac surgical case.

It was after she had stabilized in the OR that my responsibility for initiating this catastrophe really hit me. As I racked my brain trying to comprehend where I could have made a mistake, I noticed that the resuscitation team had distanced themselves from me, completing their operative tasks with intense concentration while avoiding eye contact and saying very little. The sense of teamwork that had pulled all of us together to work on a patient we knew little about was now gone, leaving an emotional vacuum in its wake. Apparently, the hospital Risk Management team had heard about the event already and had instructed everyone in the room not to say anything, or more specifically, not to say anything to me. *They* would lead the damage control.

I suppose I had expected this response, having spent years in this culture of silence. But being on the receiving end of it, particularly after a significant event such as this, was extremely unnerving and isolating. The only person who knew the patient as an individual was the orthopedic surgeon, and the memory of seeing him standing against the wall as the resuscitation unfolded only added to my sense of isolation and distress.

My instructions shortly after the event were clear: remain silent and stay away from the patient. It was in the playbook. I knew it. Everyone knew it. But part of me was deeply disturbed by this directive. I felt strongly that I should contact the husband and share what had happened. More importantly, I wanted to reassure him that his wife would be OK. I approached the surgeon and asked if he would be willing to go with me to talk with the husband. He agreed, and as we walked to the family liaison area, I imagined how the conversation would unfold. I knew it would be an emotional moment. Still, I hoped that a professional approach and an empathetic conversation around the factual account of what happened, drawing on training all physicians received to share difficult diagnoses with patients, would be well received. We would get through this.

What I didn't know was that the husband had left the hospital at his wife's request and had returned to the hospital only after the surgeon called him to let him know there had been a complication with the anesthetic, that his wife's chest had been cracked open, and that he urgently needed to come back to the hospital.

But the surgeon failed to tell me any of this as we made our way to the serene family liaison area, where the patient's husband was nowhere to be found. We asked the receptionist, who pointed us to a small conference room on the back wall where they had told him to wait for us. I prepared myself for the tough conversation as we walked to the conference room, then peered through the narrow pane of glass to observe him pacing back and forth along the edge of the wall like a caged tiger. When I opened the door, he stopped midpace, turned to me, and instantly rushed at me with a violent energy I had never experienced. I stood frozen, bracing myself for the assault, when the orthopedic surgeon suddenly leaped in front of me and tackled the husband before he could reach me.

The surgeon's large frame could barely contain the husband's fury as the man struggled to break free, inches away from me as he screamed and screamed while the surgeon pinned him against the wall. My professional demeanor quickly morphed into panic under the emotional rage emanating from the man. It was the first time in my medical career that I could see clearly, as a caregiver, how I had learned to minimize and dismiss the impact of harmful events on patients, families, and myself. Regardless of my fear, I felt compelled to break through the fury, to share the details of what had happened to his wife to reassure him that she would be OK. But everything I said, indeed my very presence, only made the husband more volatile. Against every instinct, I realized my only choice was to leave.

The surgeon was trying to calm the husband when I left. I wandered back to the operating room in a total haze, stunned by the violent confrontation. When I arrived back in the OR, it was as though nothing had happened. The OR was business as usual: people were taking care of patients, the cardiac operating room we had used was in full swing, and the only notable difference was that nobody was getting anywhere near me. As far as they were concerned, I wasn't even present.

I felt helpless, aimless, not knowing what to do when my chairman eventually found me and pulled me aside. He attempted to reassure me that there had been no error, that inadvertent intravascular injection was a rare but known complication, and that we had done everything according to the standard of care. He focused on the fact that we had pulled off a miraculous patient save and that had this patient been in any other setting, she would likely have died. He advised me to go home and rest for the remainder of the afternoon so that I could return the next day and be functional at work. His parting words of reassurance? "Even the best physicians get sued. You'll get through this."

I don't remember how I got home. There was no way to adequately share what had happened with my wife, so the lack of support and feeling of isolation continued long into the night. I couldn't figure out what I'd done or overlooked during the block placement. I couldn't escape a single surreal thought. I was numb and exhausted, yet I couldn't sleep.

The next morning, I was back in the OR as though nothing had happened. The schedulers had assigned me a full load of regional anesthetic cases, not involving popliteal fossa blocks, of course, but other regional techniques instead. I was in no condition to be caring for patients that day, and while this should have been explicitly obvious as part of the case assignment, quality, and patient safety processes, it was my direct clinical team who took the unspoken, unacknowledged corrective action. I'm thankful to this day that my exceptional teammates informally took over my clinical responsibilities to ensure my patients received good care.

No one would tell me how the patient was doing, and my need to reach out to her became more urgent as the day progressed. By the end of the day, I no longer cared about the stay-silent-stay-away directive, and at the end of my OR shift, I decided to visit her in the intensive care unit myself to confirm she was OK. But word travels faster than foot. No sooner had I made it to the cardiac ICU than I was intercepted by the critical care attending.

He took me aside and explained that the patient had regained consciousness and appeared neurologically intact, and even though she was still intubated, she was writing notes and communicating with the staff. He suggested I remain on the sidelines, expressing concern that she had experienced significant physical trauma during the resuscitation the day before and that they did not want to add potential psychological trauma on top of that—meaning me. I was the potential psychological trauma. My presence could open up a line of patient questions they would not be able to answer per the directive of silence. The intensivist said he would provide me with regular updates on her progression and suggested as a surrogate option that I speak with the patient's husband, who happened to be visiting.

Husband? I struggled momentarily against self-preservation, my urge to bolt from the unit before the man could try to pummel me again. However, my need for accountability prevailed, and I agreed to talk with the husband. Having braced myself for the worst, I was completely surprised when the husband calmly approached me with his right hand extended. I shook his hand, speechless, as he apologized for his behavior the prior day. What was happening? I was the one who had nearly killed his wife. If anyone needed to apologize, it was me. I never had the chance as he abruptly ended the conversation by asking me to stay away from his wife while she recovered. He then turned away and walked back to her ICU bed.

As much as I wanted to see her, respecting her husband's wishes became paramount. She remained in the hospital for about ten days, progressively recovering, and hard as it was, I stayed away as he'd asked. I had no debrief outlet. No way to decompress the emotional stress of the event. Anxiety and a growing desperation to talk with the patient gnawed at me. I pursued every avenue I could think of to get permission to see her, including social work, risk management, the care team, and even indirect appeals to her husband, all to no avail. Unknown to me at the time was that the hospital had told the patient the entire experience was due to an allergic reaction to the local anesthetic. This communication strategy left no possibility that this might have been attributable to medical error or iatrogenic harm.

The person who follows the crowd will usually go no further than the crowd. The person who walks alone is likely to find himself in places no one has ever seen before.

—ALBERT EINSTEIN

When the care team discharged the patient home on the tenth day, a hopelessness I'd never experienced descended on me. I was supposed to be relieved. The hospital had successfully contained any exposure of the adverse event to the public, the media, and the Department of Public Health. It was a public relations win by anyone's standards, but the win meant nothing to me. For days, isolation had chipped away at my ability to rationalize a catastrophic event into a bright side. Sitting in that chair under the crushing weight of insistent guilt and relentless thoughts, of no way to escape the moment, I finally came face-to-face with the moment. It was a breakthrough, a complete mental shutdown that left me without attachment to the situation or its outcome.

I'd compartmentalized difficult situations in the past. This wasn't that. Although I didn't understand it at the time, the emotional trauma from the event, the subsequent isolation placed on me, and my inability to morally process any of it had become the perfect storm, the perfect catalyst to force me into an unconscious surrender to the current state of affairs. Complete acceptance as I'd never known it. Almost immediately, a new direction revealed itself as though waiting for me to stop thinking long enough to hear it. *Do the right thing.* The directive rang out clear as day. Of course. The insight was beyond thought or choice. It was absolute. I needed to reach out to the patient and apologize. I had to accept full responsibility for my actions and reach out to her from human to human. It didn't matter what the outcome would be. If I were sued as a result, so be it. It was a new beginning. It was a start.

I could not contact her directly, so I decided to write her a letter with full transparency. I acknowledged the event's impact on her and her husband, at least what I had seen, and I acknowledged the event's impact on me. I apologized to her for my responsibility in performing the nerve block that led to this catastrophic outcome. I offered to share any information she might be interested in. I finished the letter by providing every piece of contact information I could think of so she could reach out to me: office phone number, pager, home address, home phone, cell phone, work, and personal email. I sent the letter.

Approximately six months would pass before I received a response.

Meanwhile, I began my clinical activities again. Although I irrevocably understood that I had done the right thing in apologizing to the patient, I now worked under a constant cloud of doubt. Doubt in myself? In the hospital? Something had changed, something unrecoverable. The hospital did not want to converse about what happened, so for now, I had to put the event behind me and overcome the residual fallout. I had to rebuild my self-confidence as an anesthesiologist and validate my credibility with my colleagues as part of the care team. But as I tried to move forward, the event kept pulling me back, mostly because I knew now that a similar event could easily happen again with no ability to anticipate or prevent it. Eventually, I succumbed to the burden of this knowledge and lost all joy in my profession. Nonclinical professional and personal activities became my sanctuaries of wellness, and eventually, I realized I needed a complete change of circumstances to regroup. In April, five months after the event, I left Boston to start a new nonclinical opportunity in Seattle with a web-enabled healthcare start-up.

I was beginning to settle into my new Seattle surroundings when I came home from work to find that my former anesthesia chairman had left me a voicemail informing me that a former patient wanted to speak with me. I knew immediately this was the patient I had harmed, and for a nanosecond, I contemplated whether I should respond. Yep, that deeply ingrained culture of blame and shame still reared its ugly head. I recognized it immediately for what it was and realized that while I may have returned to a semblance of normal routine, I was clearly not OK. I had been walking around with a big knot in my stomach, my new normal, since the event. Perhaps returning the patient's call would finally be my opportunity to connect and to do the right thing.

The call with Linda Kenney was probably the most transformative conversation of my life. It wasn't our brief recap of the event that impacted me so much as Linda's genuine interest in how I was doing emotionally. She wanted to know if I was OK. It was an awkward line of questioning. Nobody had asked me this before, and I did my best to share with her my ongoing feelings of anxiety, guilt, sadness, and isolation.

She shared with me her own experiences, how her caregivers during her immediate hospital recovery had been unemotional and guarded, but as she continued into her long-term care, the signs of emotional impact on those care team members involved in her resuscitation became clear. All of this was to ultimately tell me that she wanted to offer me her forgiveness, even though she didn't blame me for what happened. I was stunned and uplifted. It was the eight-hundred-pound weight of a gorilla jumping off my shoulders. I felt reborn. My life suddenly opened up again. If I could talk openly with the patient that I had harmed, I could talk about this event with anyone. Freedom! We ended the conversation with an agreement that we would meet in person when we were in closer geographic proximity.

Do or do not. There is no try.

—YODA

As circumstance would have it, the start-up company I worked for in Seattle filed for bankruptcy, an investment victim of the NASDAQ crash of 2000, and I ended up back at Brigham and Women's Hospital the following year. As soon as I had resettled into my BWH role, I reached out to Linda, and we met in a local coffee shop in her town.

We had not been face-to-face since before the adverse event, and it was an intense moment of closure for us. Linda shared that she had been reaching out to senior Brigham administration with a request to create an emotional support program for patients, families, and caregivers impacted by catastrophic medical events before handing me the single response she had received from hospital leadership, a legally parsed form letter that thanked her for her outreach and that affirmed the hospital's commitment to the highest standards of quality and safety. They would get back to her if the opportunity arose. "This is why patients sue," she said, still furious over the form letter.

I was so disappointed by the uncompassionate, self-protective, and irresponsible stance my hospital had taken, and I was determined to get Linda the leadership meeting she had requested. It was an immediate call to action. I told her I'd actively support her intention to create a nonprofit foundation to address the emotional support gap in the patient safety movement. Brigham's initial response was an accepted practice in many hospitals nationwide, and it was time to change that. It was time to take on healthcare.

They didn't know it was impossible, so they did it.

—MARK TWAIN

While the mission was clear, the journey Linda and I embarked on was uncharted, and it took many baby steps before everything took off. In the spring of 2002, Linda and I met with several others to brainstorm ideas for a new foundation. We emerged with a name and tagline: Medically Induced Trauma Support Services (MITSS), "To Support Healing and Restore Hope," which Linda established in

June 2002. During those first two years, my focus remained primarily within BWH, creating awareness for the needed support of caregivers involved in adverse medical events while attempting to organize a meeting between Linda and senior hospital leadership. Although progression was slow, we were fortunate to leverage the recent attention and healthcare hype around patient safety that had resulted from the Institute of Medicine's 1999 seminal publication, *To Err Is Human*, which estimated that as many as 98,000 US patient deaths per year were attributable to preventable medical error.

Similarly, the Dana Farber Cancer Institute had been proactively taking a patient-centered approach to improving patient safety following the aftermath of the iatrogenic death of Betsy Lehman, a *Boston Globe* reporter who had died as the result of a massive chemotherapy overdose. Our patient-physician team initiative around apology, disclosure, and support inspired the leadership of both the Institute of Healthcare Improvement and Dana Farber. They emerged as committed champions and supporters of our cause. Sadly, the Brigham leadership remained strongly resistant to engaging directly with MITSS. It would take a more compelling set of circumstances to change that tide.

The Road to Action

The big turning point for MITSS happened in 2004. Through the promotional efforts of the Institute of Healthcare Improvement and Dana Farber leadership, Linda and I became a public interest story for mainstream media. We ended up on the *Wall Street Journal's* radar, prompting one of their healthcare reporters to approach us regarding a feature article she was writing on the power of apology in patient harm cases. Simultaneously, we were invited by the organizers of the

National Patient Safety Foundation to present a keynote address at their annual conference in Boston in May 2004. With the keynote address and the planned *Wall Street Journal* publication falling in close sequence that month, we persuaded the Brigham leadership to finally meet with us. In contrast to what they might have expected, Linda and I showed up as compassionate and collaborative advocates for meaningful change rather than an angry team looking for restitution. We caught them off guard, perhaps offering them a window to engage around adverse events in a new cooperative way.

The National Patient Safety Foundation keynote address was another pivotal moment. We were lucky to connect with a creative innovator in presenting sensitive patient safety issues who worked with us to develop a compelling, high-impact presentation. Using a white curtain as the main prop, our presentation was choreographed to begin with me at the speaker's podium wearing my white physician coat and presenting the perioperative event with stoic professionalism. Meanwhile, Linda was behind the curtain and only visible to the audience as a shadow cast by a spotlight behind her when her speaking parts came. It was only when the story reached the convergence point of our phone call that Linda emerged from behind the screen, and the two of us sat down next to each other on stage, white coat off, human to human.

The presentation was received as both terrifying and electrifying. The keynote audience exceeded one thousand; this was the first time I had ever presented at this magnitude. It was interesting to watch the audience convene in the amphitheater with the usual camaraderie of being among inspired, kindred spirits. There was clearly a sense of great progress being made in the patient safety domain, a feeling of optimism, with success in sight. How profoundly that levity changed with our presentation. An unlikely patient-physician team had exposed the support gap, and by the end of our presentation, the audience's dead silence reflected the collective's realization that there was so much more work to be done.

That presentation thrust Linda and me onto the national and international stage. Over the next two years, we were on a traveling road show, presenting our story at a variety of hospital and conference venues through publication, radio, and television. We began to fully appreciate the magnitude of the support challenge when, after most speaking engagements, caregivers in the audience approached us with their own stories of ongoing emotional distress experienced in their practices. Everyone had a story or knew of a colleague who had fallen.

But for all the interest and inspiration that we were generating, it quickly became apparent that our mission for creating awareness and advocacy was not translating into organizational action. Typical leadership comments included, "You're doing important work. Keep it up," or "Let us know how we can help." We knew the biggest impediment to organizational action was that apology, support, and disclosure in a litigious society could be financially dangerous. It was on us to define a path through this obstacle.

Shortly after the National Patient Safety Foundation presentation, Brigham reconvened a meeting with us and offered Linda's foundation office space from which to operate independently to develop a support structure for patients and families. In addition, the Chief Medical Officer charged me and the Brigham Director of Risk Management with creating a task force to develop a support network for caregivers emotionally impacted by adverse events.

The Emergence of Caregiver Peer Support

The idea of caregiver peer support wasn't entirely new, as there were already support programs in other public service and healthcare sectors. At the time, a clinical psychologist within Boston's emergency response services had established a peer support program for the city's first responders, including police, fire department, paramedics, and emergency medical technicians. Any first responder involved in a catastrophic event was taken off service and offered emotional support. Further, we learned about an innovative support program at Kaiser Permanente in California led by their Employee Assistance Program (EAP), whose goal was to enhance caregiver access to normalized emotional support. Their tagline, "Normal people having normal reactions to abnormal events," summed it up perfectly. These programs resonated strongly with our vision, and we were fortunate to be able to visit and learn from these innovative leaders. Launching a peer support program at Brigham became my prime objective.

Our Brigham peer support task force spent two years developing a peer support training curriculum and an operational infrastructure from the ground up. We trained a cohort of anesthesiologists, surgeons, and nurses. We also developed an activation and communication strategy, a structured response capable of providing individual peer support and group interventions led by EAP. The initial use of the peer support program was predictably low, but there were a few key events that validated the need for one.

In one instance, a frail elderly patient underwent an extensive resection of a pelvic tumor with a very high risk of intraoperative mortality. The multispecialty care team did an amazing job completing the complex portion of the surgery while keeping the patient stable. However, while the team placed the final skin staples at the end of the case, the patient unexpectedly went into cardiac arrest and could not be resuscitated. The team was devastated, and we quickly pulled together a peer support group session for the team to debrief about the emotional impact. It turned out that it was the unanticipated, untimely moment of the patient's deterioration and death that tipped them over.

They thought they had pulled her through the surgery; she wasn't supposed to die when all the life-threatening steps had been successfully completed. Although the emotional impact was profound, the support opportunity enabled the team to see different perspectives on the event and to appreciate that they all felt responsible for the patient's death. Powerful team cohesion resulted from recognizing that they had all done their best and that no one was to blame. "Normal people having normal reactions to abnormal events." This case highlighted that peer support had far-reaching applications beyond adverse medical events.

Peer support continued to develop and gain acceptance slowly over the next couple of years, with the largest impediment to adoption remaining among the physicians; the need for emotional support was perceived by most as a sign of weakness, of not having the right stuff. But I was determined. We had to get past those existing cultural barriers to make this happen. I knew we had to manage physician fear with understanding and sensitivity. If nothing else, I hoped my tenacious drive would lead us down the right path and, eventually, to a widely accepted and successful peer support program. It turns out most people don't respond well to a push in an imposed direction.

Chapter 5

From Silos to Synthesis

I wore several distinct professional hats during my time at the Brigham, which in many ways functioned in silos. While MITSS and peer support had a time commitment and rhythm of their own, I was spending more than half of my professional time focused on performance and quality improvement. At the time, our orthopedic service, exceptional in surgical care as it was, was a poster child for being notoriously inefficient and inconsistent in moving patients through their perioperative care. This included all of us: surgeons, anesthesiologists, and nurses.

Delays were rampant, each perioperative team blamed the next, and overall team morale swung to pendular extremes. Attempts to develop sustainable solutions had largely failed over prior years. With my return from business school, Brigham leadership thinking was to allow me to prove my mettle. Armed with academic innovation and improvement constructs, I took on the challenge with verve and vigor. I had developed an ability to dissect complex processes and set out to understand the underlying dysfunction within our orthopedic OR pod.

Unlike the intangible insight that guided me through my adverse event with Linda, performance improvement resided squarely in operational problem solving. Without having a clear direction or even attempting to solicit the expertise of my colleagues (I foolishly thought I knew the space well enough on my own that I didn't need their input), I began to apply my learned skills in process mapping, data collection, and analytics. It quickly became evident that several key process steps contributed to throughput delays. I developed a plan that made sense to me and presented it to the interprofessional team as an established implementation plan, complete with a road map and timeline. It was a great setup for a personal learning experience.

Despite the logic of my improvement plan, very little happened. In developing the plan on my own, I had overlooked critical barriers to the identified improvement opportunities. It was a frustrating revelation of the team's intrinsic resistance to change and a sobering demonstration of how easily I had slipped into a push strategy, imposing my plan on the team, which I knew was ineffective and only intensified their resistance. I began to see the repetitive cascade of imposed change and resistance played out across organizational levels, right down to the clinician. When organizational leaders used a push strategy to "solve" systems problems, their lack of success prompted department and unit leaders to apply a similar push strategy to achieve more localized improvements. When the localized improvements inevitably fell short, individual care team members applied push strategies in the form of workarounds. Trust no one. All of this was mutually reinforcing, which created an endless cycle of worsening care conditions.

Several critical improvement elements emerged with this understanding. The importance of frontline team engagement and building trusting relationships with interprofessional teams was essential. First, spending time with everyone on the front line—OR nurses, for example—while listening to and understanding issues from their perspective established collaborative inroads to change opportunities usually considered taboo. This created frontline champions.

Second, meaningful data and analytics were paramount for accurately understanding root causes and solutions. For example, OR turnaround is typically defined as the interval between a patient leaving the OR and the next patient entering. What if we redefined turnaround time as the interval between surgery completion and the next surgery incision? Now, in addition to room cleaning and nursing setup, the turnaround would also include anesthesia and surgery prep time, which would expand the playing field. Lastly, establishing a connection between frontline initiatives and senior leadership was critical for enabling situational awareness at all levels and creating more robust guidance and support opportunities.

Ready, Set, Go: Improving Surgical Start Times

While these changes were nascent at the time, some of the throughput improvements were striking. I began to look at the surgical prep time for similar cases by orthopedic surgeons and determined that there was wide variation among them. Similarly, in reviewing the case setup time required by nursing, it became evident that there would be significant gains if they worked in parallel with the anesthesiologists in the operating room.

I continued solidifying my relationships with my surgical colleagues and with nursing and was invited to present my data at an orthopedic surgery faculty meeting, where I shared the surgical prep time by attending with the group. The data transparency resulted in an average forty-minute reduction in throughput time. Surgeons are naturally competitive, and none wanted to be at the bottom.

While there was still hesitation within nursing to relinquish control of instrument prep time, we were able to initiate pilot efforts for parallel anesthesia activity for select case types. Finally, I was able to leverage my connections with leadership to make front-end challenges visible and garner more involved guidance and support to create sustained improvements. It was the beginning of a collective appreciation of the value derived from data-driven, collaborative problem solving. There was a win in it for everyone.

Taming the Wild West: Out-of-OR Procedures

As the intensity of the orthopedic improvement efforts began to taper, I started to look for another improvement initiative. In 2004, I was asked to serve as an internal consultant to the Chief Medical Officer to assess and develop recommendations for what, at the time, was a dramatic and poorly understood increase in the number of interventional procedures taking place outside of the operating room environment. Minimally invasive interventional techniques had opened entirely new alternatives to surgical care and specialty services, including cardiology, interventional radiology, and gastroenterology, which had all significantly expanded their out-of-OR procedures. Hospital leadership had limited information on procedure type and case volumes and was particularly concerned about the quality and safety of the care being delivered.

I eagerly embraced this initiative and spent long hours observing the different interventional areas, building relationships and trust with faculty and staff, mapping their care processes, and collecting relevant data on procedures, case volumes, and patient throughput. I was impressed and alarmed by what I saw, particularly from my vantage as an anesthesiologist. The deployed technology and the types of interventions being performed were incredible, far beyond what I had initially imagined.

Patients who would have been considered extremely high-risk or noncandidates for conventional surgery now had treatment alternatives. However, it gave me great pause to note the lack of appreciation of the risk that patients were subjected to during these non-OR interventions. The minimally invasive approaches deflected attention from the magnitude of the actual interventions, which created the false impression that patients did not require comprehensive preprocedural assessment. Further, the escalated intensity of the out-of-OR procedures and increased case length no longer aligned with the sedation guidelines for interventionalists.

For example, certain patients with significant gallbladder obstruction would be taken to the interventional radiology suite for balloon dilatation. The interventionalist would provide the patient with sedation according to the guidelines, which worked well until the balloon had to be inflated, causing extreme transient pain. In the absence of an anesthesiologist, the interventionalist's only option would be to give a large dose of a guideline-approved opioid, such as fentanyl, immediately prior to inflating the balloon. This would barely provide the necessary pain control during the inflation and would promptly put the patient into respiratory arrest when the balloon was deflated. The interventional radiology service would then activate the hospital's Code Green (airway) response, which would emergently summon anesthesia to resuscitate the patient. What's worse, this process had been normalized as the standard of care!

There were many other examples of Wild West out-of-OR care, and it was clear that many procedures needed anesthesia evaluation and coverage. In addition to demonstrating the clinical need for anesthesia coverage, it also turned out that there were at least as many out-of-OR procedures as OR surgeries, about twenty-five thousand per year, and this would require dedicated resources and a governance structure to be sustainable. Given the urgent need for improvement, I was given yet another title, Director of Non-OR Anesthesia (NORA), and charged with building the service model.

The development of non-OR anesthesia was a formidable task on several fronts. Culturally, the traditionally anesthesia-independent interventional services balked at the perceived excess caution being imposed on them, which threatened their practice autonomy. Anesthesia involvement was also perceived as highly inefficient, an added complexity hindering access and throughput. Anesthesiologists were similarly averse to the non-OR environment because it removed them from their comfort zone, the OR, and introduced a completely new approach to anesthesia care.

Further, many interventional suites had not been outfitted with standard anesthesia monitoring and equipment, which intensified safety concerns. Finally, there were financial barriers to delivering anesthesia services because the insurance payers did not yet recognize the non-OR environment as a standard practice area for anesthesiologists. Suffice it to say that all the improvement methodologies and techniques I had in my repertoire were maximally challenged to move this forward. I could appreciate more fully that as difficult as it was to facilitate improvement teams by understanding the current state and improvement options, it would take far greater effort to move stakeholders to accountability and action.

Without committed leadership guidance and support, implementation of sustainable change was limited. While hospital leadership was intent on creating a safer, more structured, and more efficient non-OR environment, the willingness to disrupt autonomous clinical practice and challenge clinical leadership domains was tepid. As someone who felt driven with an urgency to transform care, this drawn-out process and slow progression continued to frustrate and wear me down.

Vision without execution is hallucination.

—UNKNOWN

The profound resistance to change continued to show up as one of the biggest barriers within both the peer-support efforts and the care-improvement initiatives. The underlying system dysfunction that we trained and practiced in, which was frustrating and inefficient as it was, was our normalized work environment. It was a familiar stomping ground; vigilance was our guardrail, and we were all masters of the workaround. It had become the devil that we knew.

It was much easier to remain comfortably uncomfortable in known surroundings with functional makeshift processes and tools than to foray into uncertain territory empty-handed, trusting that the newly designed systems and services would work. Since most new processes arrived via an unwanted push, they never seemed to work. At the cultural core of healthcare, effective care delivery, quality and patient safety, and personal well-being were all individual responsibilities. Resistance to change was frightening and personal.

Fear was a powerful barrier to executing even the best-laid plans, and it was so easy and desirable to fall into a push mode to move through this. For the different improvement tracks I pursued in peer support and care improvement, the overlapping resistance to change began to pull me in a new direction of inquiry. Surely, there was a connection between the two, and as I set out to find it, a unique opportunity presented itself.

Let's not forget that the little emotions are the great captains of our lives, and we obey them without realizing it.

—VINCENT VAN GOGH

In the spring of 2005, a friend of Linda's reached out inquiring whether her coaching program facilitator, David Dibble, could meet us, as he was very intrigued by our story and work. Linda and I agreed to meet, and it quickly became evident that our approach and objectives authentically inspired David. He shared that he was doing work in professional and personal improvement using his approach called the New Agreements in the Workplace,[3] which combined universal

---

3   David Dibble, *The New Agreements in the Workplace: Releasing the Human Spirit* (The Emeritus Group, 2002).

systems principles and the Four Agreements, the personal transformation principles of Don Miguel Ruiz.

I was unfamiliar with the Four Agreements, but I was immediately pulled by the connection of systems and human dynamics as key components of sustainable improvement. David explained that he had studied with Don Miguel Ruiz for eight years, which triggered additional interest in me regarding my own experience following Linda's event. Perhaps his work could provide more answers. Sensing my interest, David invited me to consider participating in one of his five-day New Agreements training sessions scheduled for later that year. He had started consulting with a couple of community hospitals and intimated that the training participants would be from these hospitals.

I participated in David's training in the autumn and was part of a group of healthcare professionals from two hospitals in Michigan and New Mexico. Although I had participated in quality and safety improvement seminars before, David's curriculum and training approach provided a distinct and compelling perspective and depth to systems thinking and human dynamics. Where most improvement workshops provided cursory attention to the importance of systems, focusing largely on the application of improvement tools, his New Agreements curriculum underscored the importance of systems principles to understanding systems interconnectivity and user influence.

For example, David was a strong proponent of W. Edwards Deming, one of the founding fathers of performance improvement through his work with Toyota, who had defined the "94% Rule," which states more than 94 percent of outcomes, good or bad, are the result of systems, not individual effort.[4] In addition to shifting attention and blame for system dysfunction

---

4   W. Edwards Deming, *Out of the Crisis* (Cambridge: The MIT Press, 2000), 270.

away from people, the applied principle also validated the emotional stress experienced by the users of these broken systems. This was a natural segue for the concurrent need to focus on human behavior to create sustainable change. Don Miguel Ruiz's Four Agreements, (1) be impeccable with your word, (2) don't take anything personally, (3) don't make assumptions, and (4) always do your best, served as David's anchor for understanding and guiding individual and team behavior.

The constructs of systems principles and human behavior echoed strongly, and I could see how they manifested in the work that I was doing at the Brigham. The tipping point to becoming a champion of the New Agreements occurred when David shared his emotional content brainstorming method for leveraging emotional energy to identify systems issues and to narrow them down to critical 20 percent focus areas based on Pareto's Law, which states that 20 percent of system inputs create 80 percent of the results. Suddenly, I could see how these vital elements that I had been applying to my work in relative isolation could be integrated to advance the teams through change resistance toward sustained improvement.

I returned to the Brigham from the training energized and ready to apply what I had learned only to discover that the application of emotional content brainstorming was much more nuanced than I had thought, and I was not effective in facilitating its use. I decided to learn David's facilitating approach directly, and over the following year, I carved out time to shadow David on two of his healthcare engagements. This observation period was eye-opening, an incredible experience demonstrating David's mastery of team facilitation and the powerful team synergies created through systems-based problem solving and leveraging emotional stress.

The frontline improvement workgroups were developing profound breakthroughs to operational challenges that had been stagnant for years. I also noted once again that sustainable change did not occur without the requisite leadership commitment, guidance, and support and that the New Agreements methodology was not a magic bullet for transformation. But it was certainly a significant step in the right direction.

It was clear that mastering team facilitation was one of the most important success factors in applying the New Agreements method. I needed to develop a deep understanding of human dynamics principles and a keen sensitivity to the emotional energy associated with change. David had appeared in the right place at the right time to pursue this, and together, we created a one-year New Agreements fellowship position that I served from 2007 to 2008 while continuing to work part time at the Brigham. I shared my New Agreements experience with a few of my close Brigham perioperative nursing colleagues. Through these connections, I set up a six-month improvement engagement with David and me as consultants. This engagement proved to be another pivotal learning experience.

The Case of the Dull Scissors: Trusting the Process

The perioperative nursing service struggled with increasing surgical volume in significant resource constraints and throughput inefficiencies. Nursing morale was at an all-time low, reflecting an urgent need for change. We started our initial emotional content brainstorm with a disgruntled and dubious group of nurses, leading the session with a general question around issues and concerns related to delivering great perioperative nursing care.

After an initial period of awkward silence, David masterfully enticed the group to open up. Before we knew it, we were furiously capturing a catharsis of issues on multiple sheets of flip chart paper for all to see, probably for the first time. Of the major themes they distilled from this expansive list, the nurses insisted that dull surgical scissors be selected as their most pressing improvement opportunity.

David and I looked at each other, somewhat dumbfounded. *Dull scissors?* The typical logic-based response would have dismissed this focus area as an emotional anomaly, a distraction, but the methodology dictated that we follow their emotionally informed path. Trusting the process, we established a dull scissors workgroup and proceeded down the analytic path to understand the root causes of the problem.

To our great surprise, the dull-scissors trail led the workgroup to a vast opportunity within central sterile processing, where years of well-intended problem firefighting and uncoordinated improvement efforts had created numerous lapses in instrument inventory and throughput management. Over the engagement period, the workgroup developed a comprehensive improvement proposal with a corresponding business case for change, which projected a return on investment of $750,000. Inspired by the potential output of their improvement efforts and the impact that their solution could have on their daily work routines, the workgroup charged us with presenting their proposal to senior nursing leadership. The meeting did not go as planned.

Commitment vs. Attachment: An Important Distinction

During the six months of the engagement that had preceded our final meeting with senior nursing leaders, the frontline teams had evolved from disenchanted and disempowered followers to proactively empowered change agents. They were accustomed to being on the receiving end of leadership directives, and we had offered them an alternative approach to improvement that tapped their collective genius.

David and I were clear that the proposal presentation was a critical moment that would test nursing leadership's appetite for change. Our presentation on the proposed improvements for central sterile processing and a few more perioperative improvements that other workgroups had developed met with minimal impact. Due to the usual financial constraints and the challenge of moving beyond the pervasive firefighting mindset of reactive problem solving, it was clear that none of the proposed initiatives would be substantively supported.

I was not surprised by the response, as it was the institutional norm, but I was saddened for the nurses who had put so much effort into this work, all for naught. I knew this was probably one of the last chances anyone would have to engage these nurses with the same energy and intent. It was disheartening for us both, but I understood and could detach from the outcome, as I already had years of experience doing exactly that in my clinical arena.

Another important lesson emerged from this engagement and my overall time as the New Agreements fellow. As intuitive as it seemed and as synergistic as it was, integrating emotional energy with systems-based improvement principles was a combustible mixture requiring careful management. I repeatedly found that team participants and leaders became very edgy by including qualitative inputs to improvement approaches that were typically quantitative. Their discomfort was often exacerbated when the Four Agreements were used to explain the relationship of emotional content to change, principles that unintentionally suggested a spiritual connection and challenged personal beliefs. I saw the connection of emotional peer support to my systems redesign work but recognized that the explanation was not to be found in ideology or theology. Like insight, it was deeper and much more basic, and I didn't quite have my finger on it yet. It felt just out of my reach.

But as the framework of a new methodology began to take shape in my mind, I was excited to roll up my sleeves and build it out further as my fellowship time with David came to closure.

Chapter 6

From Covert to Overt

Good teams become great ones when the members trust each other enough to surrender the "me" for the "we."

—PHIL JACKSON

I had reached a point in my clinical redesign work where my efforts for creating accelerated and profound change were not budging the conservative pace that large academic medical centers like the Brigham embraced. Despite all that I had learned and could accomplish with frontline team engagement and systems-based problem solving, I was repeatedly confronted with change inertia, particularly at the leadership level. As I tried to navigate out of the change doldrums, searching for a way forward, I realized that I was not exempt from the systems principles and emotional stressors I was addressing within the improvement teams.

I was part of the established leadership system, and I stood very little chance of changing it on my own. Deming's 94% Rule in action.

Awareness of this was pivotal, and I landed in a field of calm as the solution lit up in front of me. It had been *my* expectations for change that were creating my stress as they clashed with the existing leadership paradigm, not the other way around.

Understanding my responsibility for my discontent dissolved it, and I realized it was time to move on, to leave the Brigham. I knew it might take a minute for the next opportunity to show up, and in the meantime, I could engage in my work in a new way, appreciating that the pace and magnitude of change would be determined by the organization's willingness to partake. There was no conflict or contradiction in offering all I had without expectation or contingency for a particular outcome. *Committed and not attached.* With this liberating insight, I kept my eyes open for professional opportunities where my passion and developing expertise in care improvement and redesign would be sought after and leveraged.

My Brigham tenure ended in August 2008 when I was offered a position at Partners Harvard Medical International as a Director for Global Programs. They were involved in a multimillion-dollar health system development project in Dubai and were looking to expand their quality improvement capacity there as well as globally. This was a dream come true, an opportunity to combine my systems improvement skills with my passion for international travel. I would actively guide and support the development of Dubai Healthcare City's quality and safety infrastructure and serve on a Partners quality improvement team that worked with hospitals in Asia and Eastern Europe to prepare them for Joint Commission international accreditation. This was a big career transition, marking the end of my clinical anesthesiology practice and eliminating my clinical financial safety net.

The following five years at Partners International were highly formative and served to define my improvement methodology with greater clarity. Many of the improvement elements I had learned during my years at the Brigham and my time with David had been revised, refined, and augmented. I was much more organized and saw the different components as an integrated whole. I understood the intimate connection that qualitative emotional peer support had to quantitative systems improvement methods. I'd embraced the model of effective systems improvement being analogous to patient-centered care; in both settings, one had to be attentive to the issues and concerns of the impacted individuals to arrive at the correct diagnosis and treatment.

The key attribute of this analogy was being attentive to both the emotional qualitative and the operational quantitative inputs of those impacted. The synergy between the two was magic. Although I knew that the emotional component would likely require an ongoing inconspicuous submersion during engagements, its importance and distinctive role in creating conditions for sustained high-impact outcomes would necessitate moving it out of the covert realm where it was incubating. The next step on the development path would bring it another step closer to the surface.

Love what you do. Love who you do it with. Love who you do it for.

—THE CHARTIS GROUP

During my final year at Partners Healthcare International, the mission focus shifted away from quality and safety improvement, and my expertise in system redesign was no longer considered essential; in September 2013, I was made redundant. It was disappointing, but the circumstance coincided with my having recently remarried and a desire to rebalance my professional and personal priorities. This was again a moment of great uncertainty. As urgent as the situation was, I had become comfortable understanding that the right opportunity would show up without overthinking it.

Things always worked out the way they were supposed to. Several months later, my former Partners International COO and mentor contacted me regarding a possible job opportunity with the Chartis Group, a smaller consulting firm focused primarily on serving the US healthcare provider space. One of the Chartis managing directors he knew had expressed interest in expanding their healthcare performance practice with physicians to enhance their clinical expertise and credibility. With my interest piqued, my mentor arranged an email introduction, and within short order, I was interviewing with Chartis for a position. The interview process went well, and in April 2014, I accepted the position of Clinical Associate Principal (AP), the first role of its kind at Chartis.

I had landed another incredible opportunity to learn and advance my approach to complex problem solving and clinical practice transformation. Chartis was passionate about its people and clients and committed to reshaping healthcare with high-impact results. Everyone at Chartis authentically embraced its vision and mission for healthcare transformation, and I immediately felt like a welcomed addition to the close-knit family.

My next four years at Chartis provided me with several significant professional development opportunities, not the least of which involved deepening my critical thinking, client management, and communications competencies. Chartis raised the bar well beyond my prior level of function by further underscoring the importance of analytic rigor, serving as a trusted advisor to senior client leadership, and synthesizing complex challenges into compelling messages that "told the client's story" and inspired them to action. It was humbling to expose my consulting gaps, and at the same time, I saw it as a great opportunity to push the envelope. Every Chartis team member's commitment and enthusiasm for each other and our clients' success created an intense energy that voraciously fueled collaborative problem solving and solution development.

My role as a clinical AP gave me some wiggle room to introduce some of my prior improvement methodologies into the standard Chartis approach to performance improvement. Interestingly, the complementary strength of my problem-solving approach typically manifested at the front end of our engagements because of the typical pattern of several-week delays that would occur while we waited for clients to respond to our data requests. While my Chartis teammates would be caught in a relative holding pattern, I would go into the clinical frontline care areas and spend time with the different care team professionals, including physicians, nurses, and pharmacists, rounding with them on patients and observing their overall work patterns.

In contrast to popular executive work rounds, which provided brief and somewhat staged flybys for senior hospital leaders to receive cursory exposure to hospital service area successes and challenges, my approach was to assimilate as a fellow clinician and to observe what was *actually* going on rather than what was *supposed* to happen. I named my frontline observations CLUE Rounds (Connect, Listen, Understand, Engage). Unlike my nonclinical Chartis teammates, I quickly leveraged my credibility as a provider, spoke their clinical language, and asked questions about their issues and concerns as a peer, which built relationships and trust.

The units became my trusted "patients." By being attentive and listening to their problems, I began to identify and understand specific areas for improvement and started creating conditions for effective care team engagement. By the time our client data request became available, it was often the case that my CLUE Rounding had already identified key focus areas for our engagement and that the data analytics served more as target validation and clarification rather than being directional. On top of that, our Chartis team now had paved access to frontline care teams, which enabled our whole team to be incorporated as trusted colleagues. It was a novel synergy of qualitative and quantitative inputs that strengthened our collaborative approach and created conditions for strong and sustained results.

In keeping with the interconnectivity of systems, it was not uncommon for CLUE Rounds to expose critical unanticipated improvement opportunities well beyond the initial scope of the planned engagement. In one instance, we were working with a large neonatal intensive care unit (NICU) at a major academic medical center where we had been asked to develop solutions to several significant nursing challenges resulting from a prior redesign of their unit from a traditional open floor care model to one with private rooms. This resulted in a profound shift in how nurses interacted and supported each other, from being highly visible and collaborative to much more partitioned and isolated.

Initially, our focus was nurse-centered and structural, and this was certainly a key challenge. However, in conducting a series of CLUE Rounds with the nurses, the nurse practitioners, and the physicians, we began to uncover the disruptive impact of the overall NICU redesign extending across the entire care team. We were suddenly thrust into a situation that required a much broader approach across the multiprofessional care teams, including the pediatric residents. Our subsequent deeper dive into understanding their current state using process mapping, data analytics, and ongoing CLUE Rounds resulted in an improvement plan that included a new training curriculum and onboarding program for nursing, a revised coverage model and a scheduling method for all care team professionals, and an overhaul of the pediatric resident NICU training rotation. Not only did CLUE Rounds serve to uncover a much larger improvement footprint, but they also became an essential modality for establishing a support platform for the emotional stress embedded in all this change.

As a Chartisan, I was fortunate to serve in various performance improvement and redesign engagements, mostly at hospitals within large academic health systems. Many of our engagements focused on common care delivery challenges, such as patient capacity, access, and throughput. For all the quantitative and process-driven improvement needs, it was so striking how much associated emotional stress was embedded in the challenges once we were attentive to them. The more we worked on these engagements, the more obvious they became.

Most consulting engagement requests arose from organizational C-suite leaders and generally focused on specific operations or finances. While conventional consulting methodologies might indirectly or coincidentally touch the emotional element, our incorporation of CLUE Rounding intentionally addressed emotional stressors and often gave senior leaders a novel appreciation of its importance. While the core improvement drivers of cost, quality, safety, productivity, and performance remained a high priority, a shift in C-suite focus to faculty and staff wellness became increasingly apparent in my latter years at Chartis.

Where wellness had always been viewed as a secondary "nice to have" improvement outcome, the worsening crisis of staffing shortages, attrition, and burnout elevated wellness as a prime focus. The timing was now right for the work I had been doing and the methodology I had been refining to make a big splash. I just needed the right engagement to show up.

The CLUE to Hospital Medicine Redesign

The right opportunity presented itself in February 2017 when I was assigned to serve as the engagement lead for a five-week assessment of the Hospital Medicine service at the University of Alabama at Birmingham Health System (UABHS). Over the prior decade, the Hospital Medicine (HM) service had grown significantly to meet the demand for dedicated acute inpatient care. What started as a small nonacademic group practice had reached a size that no longer aligned with the original care model, which resulted in increased provider dissatisfaction and very low engagement scores on a recent UABHS employee survey. Hospital senior leadership recognized the need for a greater understanding of the problem and the timeliness for implementing a sustainable solution.

The qualitative nature of the engagement request offered very little in the way of usual data-driven analytic guidance, which made it the perfect venue for CLUE Rounding. With the trust and confidence of my Chartis director, I set forth on my mission to understand the current state of the HM service at the front end of care. The assessment period went by very quickly. In addition to meetings with key stakeholders across the multiple medical and surgical specialties that interacted with Hospital Medicine, I spent multiple hours conducting CLUE Rounds in a variety of care settings with a broad range of HM caregivers, including physicians, advanced practice professionals (APPs), clinical care coordinators, and unit nurses.

The objective I always shared with those I was observing was to understand their workflow process and listen to any issues and concerns they chose to share related to daily care delivery. I was clear that I was there to learn and had no agenda or action plan in my back pocket. I would spend at least half the day with a care team member, a time interval that lent itself to lowering their guard and authentically sharing their perspectives and ideas.

Between the stakeholder meetings and CLUE Rounds, the amount of information being shared was overwhelming, and I had realized with prior engagements that, as counterintuitive as it might appear, it was not helpful for me to attempt to document all of this. Further, I did not want to be furiously taking notes while rounding and risk being perceived as a disingenuous neutral colleague. After my adverse event with Linda in 1999, I developed an ability to see complex systems challenges holistically, a phenomenon where my letting go of concentrated effort created a flash synthesis of the big picture. I couldn't predict when it would happen, but I understood it would happen at the right time.

Things clicked for me about three weeks into the assessment, and out of the functional problem that emerged, I identified six key areas that needed to be addressed to move Hospital Medicine in a new direction. It had become evident that the Hospital Medicine service delivered great patient care. Through its rapid growth and prioritized need to cover increasing inpatient demand, it had evolved into a model replete with mission ambiguity and misaligned incentives.

There was an opportunity to redefine HM's purpose and, from there, to develop a more integrated leadership model in alignment with UABHS's tripartite academic mission (clinical care, education, and research), clarify working relationships with other hospital specialties whose patients HM cared for in-hospital, and create conditions for a more team-oriented collaborative care model, which included coverage model changes, patient cohorts on units, and financial model redesign.

Our CLUE round findings and stakeholder meetings enabled us to identify validating data sources, providing a well-rounded qualitative and quantitative assessment report with targeted recommendations for change. Our presentation to UAB hospital leadership was well received, and the scope of the opportunity was no doubt much larger than they had anticipated.

It was clear that the HM redesign needed to happen soon, and it was apparent to all that they did not have internal leadership resources to dedicate to this endeavor. With the relationships I had established within Hospital Medicine and the deep understanding of their service challenges, hospital leadership asked whether I could continue serving as the interim administrative leader to guide and support the HM redesign development and implementation. Since the opportunity aligned with our Chartis mission and I was enthusiastically supportive, we agreed to extend the engagement for another year.

I was effectively seconded to serve as interim vice president for Hospital Medicine for the continuation of the work. Though challenging, our success in collaboratively transforming the HM service during the next twelve months was deeply satisfying and created the opportunity for me to transition from Chartis to UABHS as their inaugural Chief Clinical Transformation Officer. I was now positioned to integrate all I had learned through trials and tribulations, observation, and understanding into a cohesive paradigm for transformation. The opportunity now was to make the change methodology simple, user-friendly, and accessible so we could use it for other redesign initiatives at UABHS and share it broadly across the healthcare continuum. Game on.

SECTION II

Looking to Understand

Chapter 7

The Secret Sauce to Transformation

If you want to go fast, go alone. If you want to go far, go together.

—AFRICAN PROVERB

How often have you been asked to participate in meetings or problem-solving sessions where very few relevant or actionable items emerge? A senior leader or manager might lead meetings with a predetermined solution, you and other participants may be hesitant to contribute to the conversation because of the pecking order, different opinions and solutions might be put forward, challenged, and defended, and at the end, you are left with a lot of disagreement, frustration, and inertia. When this happens in repetition, that feeling of dread and meeting fatigue in being asked to be part of a problem-solving team "one more time" is enough for many to refuse outright or to show up with fisticuffs.

It is very common for my team to be invited to guide and support a complex problem-solving engagement after numerous prior unsuccessful attempts and to be met with this dynamic. We have one chance to demonstrate that our approach will be different from what teams have previously experienced, one chance to transition teams from cynical confrontation to curiosity. If we can't pique team interest, pulling them together for a second chance can be very difficult.

I've spent much time reflecting on the secret sauce to effective problem solving and achieving sustained high-impact results. Why do some teams we work with soar above the weather with clear visibility while others get caught in persistent stormy turbulence? I can now see that the system's problems we often try to solve are intimately related to the conflict in understanding what is going on and identifying what solutions will work. There is a reinforcing connection between individual, team, and organizational conflict that directly influences our ability to achieve sustained improvement for all. While many barriers and conflicts surface in the problems we tackle, there are also innate convergence points where individuals and teams resist or refuse to take action on the improvements we've collectively identified. Why is that? Let's take a deeper dive into understanding the nature of conflict.

We Innately Associate Problems with Conflict

If we look honestly at our daily lives, personal and professional, we will notice that life is full of problems and conflicts. Most of the time, problems and conflicts show up as one and the same, and it is fascinating to see how this routinely reveals itself in our conversations. For example, we commonly confront one another with questions and phrases like: "What's your problem?" "You're wrong!" "I disagree!" "It's your fault!" "What were you thinking?"

We have expressions that offer hope and resilience for enduring conflict: "Look on the bright side." "It'll get better next year." "Embrace the suck." "It's a rite of passage." Finally, we have catchphrases affirming that conflict will be our lasting travel companion, including: "Let's agree to disagree." "Let's compromise." "Let's negotiate." "Let's legislate." "Let's escalate." I'm sure you can think of many others. Given how common and easily we entangle problems with conflict, I attempted to separate the two by looking up the root and definition of the words in question.

The Latin/Greek root *problema* is "a task, that which is proposed, a question"; the *New Oxford American Dictionary* definition is "a matter or situation regarded as unwelcome or harmful and needing to be dealt with and overcome." It's evident that the word "problem" doesn't explicitly have conflict in its dictionary meaning. For our purposes, let's consider a problem as an objective or quantitative functional challenge that is fact-based. A personal example might be preparing for snow removal following a major snowstorm. Providing patients, families, and hospital employees with access to flu shots might be a work-related problem. In both cases, our approach to understanding and solving these problems is factual, based on what is actually taking place.

The root of the word "conflict" comes from the Latin *conflictus*, which means "to strike together or to be in opposition." The current dictionary definition is "a serious disagreement or argument, typically a protracted one; a difference of opinion." In contrast to our definition of a functional, fact-based problem, a conflict highlights subjective differences in ideas between people, which create confrontation and resistance.

We can think of a conflict as a subjective or qualitative personal challenge resulting from comparisons involving status, values, and expectations. It's important to recognize that conflict is based on abstraction, where we deal with ideas rather than facts. Agreeing on what time my teenage daughter's weekend curfew should be now that she's driving can be a conflict.

Establishing an agreed-upon scope of clinical practice for physicians and nurse practitioners in the same specialty can be a conflict. In these scenarios, resolving conflict is driven by reconciling differing individual or group values, ideas, and opinions. These can be emotional lightning rods and exceedingly difficult.

IS A PROBLEM ALWAYS A CONFLICT?

As we observed in the previous examples, there is generally no conflict if we can address a functional problem from a factual standpoint. However, conflict ensues if we overlay a functional problem with comparative opinions and conclusions based on our differing values, expectations, and ideas on how that problem should be solved. The functional problem becomes secondary to the conflict, and we are now more focused on resolving the conflict; the conflict has unwittingly become the primary problem, and we are more preoccupied with what we think *should be*, which is an idea rather than understanding *what is*, which is factual. Here's a simple example of a functional problem becoming a conflict when ideas based on value and expectation are introduced:

Simple Math: $4 \times 5 = 20$ (No value judgment: "I know this" –
No conflict)

Simple Math: $4 \times 5 = 20$ (Value judgment: "I know this. You
should know this!" – Conflict)

Complex Math: $x2 - 8x + 15 = 0$ (No value judgment: "I don't
know this" – No conflict)

Complex Math: $x2 - 8x + 15 = 0$ (Value judgment: "I *should*
know this" – Conflict)

Notice how the functional math problem remains unchanged and how the focus shifts to personal conflict when introducing a value-based comparison. Consider how often we compare and opine, injecting "should be" into our daily interactions and activities. How does one turn snow removal into a conflict? Easy! We take this simple task and ask ourselves: "Why should I do it myself when I have a fully capable teenager who should be able to use the snow blower?" And just like that, we're riled up and frustrated, which sets us up for confrontational problem solving.

FRAGMENTATION CREATES CONFLICT

Subjective comparison divides or fragments problems into what we think *is* and what we think *should be*, creating personal conflict. When we come together as a group, our expression of differing priorities, values, and expectations magnifies the fragmentation and conflict, usually making problems worse rather than better.

I was once on a family hike in Sedona, Arizona, where we got disoriented as we returned to our car. We all thought we knew the correct direction, all different, and we worked ourselves up in a heated argument trying to convince each other which way to go. One person would march off decisively, and the others would angrily follow. We took turns leading each other around in circles several times this way before coincidentally finding the parking lot.

Another time, I was working as a surgical intern evaluating an emergency room patient with a mass under the collarbone near the neck. The location of the mass made identifying the correct specialty service for admitting the patient difficult: Should the patient go to the head and neck surgeons, the thoracic surgeons, or the general surgeons? Each surgical team thought the other team should admit the patient, and after several hours of indecisive swirl and hoopla, we admitted the patient to the nonsurgical Hospital Medicine service to end the stalemate; the surgical teams would need to figure it out later. Talk about being patient-centered!

Why does fragmentation play such a key role in creating conflict? The definition of fragment is "a small part broken or separated off something; an isolated or incomplete part of something." We all show up with partial information, and conflict results when we try to understand the whole problem based on our separated or incomplete perspectives. Since no one has a complete knowledge-based understanding of any complex problem, we innately fill the knowledge gaps with our ideas, theories, and hypotheses. We generally cling to our fragmented points of view and spend a lot of time and effort trying to convince others that we are right and that they should follow. This creates confusion and conflicting interpretations of what we think is going on, with the blind leading the blind. It's like trying to assemble a one-thousand-piece puzzle without having the complete picture— we all think our piece is most important and think we know what the result should look like.

UNDERSTANDING THE NATURE OF FRAGMENTATION AND CONFLICT

As we observed at the beginning of the chapter, problems and conflict are a steady state occurrence for all of us. Let's take a moment to inquire into the nature of fragmentation and conflict and see whether we can understand its deep-seated root. From the very beginning, we inherit traditions, build mental models, and create images that define our identity: who we think we are and what we value. My father was Dutch, my mother is German, and I built on that heritage to shape my worldview. I was raised Christian, which imparts its moral code of conduct; I went to Amherst College and leveraged its reputation for academic excellence. We establish ourselves as individuals comprised of a mosaic of ideas and images, many of which contradict each other, and our fragmented identities create further division and isolation relative to each other—I think I am different from you.

Although we emphasize the importance of individuality, it can become frightening and lonely to live in an environment with constant change and uncertainty where we are against the world. As we go about our daily routines, we become our relative reference point of stability, trying to make sense of our surroundings and connect where we can. We filter, classify, and compare our experiences against our values, accumulated knowledge, and expectations, always looking to identify things that align or challenge.

When we find something or someone with common interests that provides pleasure or security, we pursue it further and maybe join a group. For example, when I moved back from Africa to Amherst, Massachusetts, in eighth grade, I signed up for youth football. I loved being part of organized sports, and being on a team was also an opportunity to make friends with my teammates with similar interests.

When we experience something that doesn't align with our values and expectations, we may feel uncomfortable or threatened, and we are usually in conflict; our perception of what *is* going on is not what *should* be happening. We are conflicted and experience emotional stress, including frustration, anger, sadness, helplessness, and isolation. My observation of wrong-site surgery in chapter 2 when I was in medical school is a good example; that just wasn't supposed to happen in healthcare, and there didn't seem to be any way for me or anyone else to do anything about it.

It's sobering to see how much fragmentation or division we all experience at multiple levels based on status, values, and ideals and the conflict this creates—nationalities: Ukraine and Russia; ideologies: capitalism and communism; religion: Hindu and Muslim; sex: male and female; politics: republican and democrat; professions: white collar and blue collar; sports team rivalries: New York Yankees and Boston Red Sox. The list is endless. Healthcare is also rife with division and conflict—leadership roles: administrative and clinical; position: frontline staff and senior leaders; expertise: general practitioner and specialist; scope of practice: physician and nurse practitioner. In short, we are all perfectly wired to fragment our lives and create conflict in most of what we do.

HOW DO FRAGMENTATION AND CONFLICT AFFECT PROBLEM SOLVING?

While our fragmented approach to life and way of thinking is common to everyone, awareness and understanding of these fundamental processes are often overlooked; it's so much a part of who we are that it becomes imperceptible, like a ring or wristwatch worn every day. Through our qualitative comparisons and interpretations, we respond reactively to the conflict we create by focusing on what we think matters most to ourselves rather than addressing the common functional problem. It's all about Number One—me, my team, my organization.

We focus on the visible manifestations of conflict and typically try to alleviate the immediate effects rather than understanding its root cause, aiming to relieve the associated symptoms of distress. Our preoccupation with conflict resolution often exacerbates the underlying problem complexity and our perceived lack of control, which reinforces our pattern of creating self-centered solutions. For example, let's say my family and I are going on a family vacation on an airline with which only I have top-tier frequent flier status. It's a full flight, and we don't want to check our luggage, so when my "elite" boarding zone is called, I bring my seven family members with me to the podium and request that they be allowed to board as well. The gate agents give me a scouring look, but it's easier for them to acquiesce, so they let us board. You can imagine the reaction the other passengers are feeling as well. Conflict.

When we show up with our individual interpretations of what is going on and no one is really interested in listening to anyone else's point of view, the easiest path forward is for all of us to act on what we individually or factionally think *should be.* Our future-focused abstraction leaves our bandwidth for what is *actually* going on—the functional problem—in the dust. We are now firmly entrenched in the domain of our opinions, hypotheses, and ideas.

Our fragmented efforts to achieve our ideals often result in self-serving jumps to solutions or workarounds with suboptimal results, improving our position to the detriment of others. This rarely addresses the root of the problem. In the travel example above, I solved my immediate conflict by leveraging my airline status at other passengers' inconvenience, and the underlying functional problem of limited carry-on baggage capacity wasn't touched. When we all start doing this, our collective suboptimization interconnects fragmentation and conflict across multiple levels (individual, team, and organization), intensifying the conflict and problem. Everyone does what's best for them, and we no longer see the root problem.

Let's go further using this example. If you travel a lot as I do, you can see how functional problems with different fragmented solutions conflict with each other across multiple levels, creating unintended consequences. At the organizational level, airlines are always looking to minimize cost and maximize revenue, so they charge passengers for checking in luggage. Their focus on maximizing profit makes carry-on baggage capacity worse.

In addition to the basic convenience of carry-on luggage, passengers are now further incented with their own cost savings; more passengers arrive with carry-on bags. Airlines are always focused on customer loyalty, so they create frequent flier programs and credit card opportunities for passengers to get preferential boarding. This segments passengers into groups at lesser and greater risk for carry-on baggage challenges. Most airlines create further segmentation by partitioning the cabins by the ticket cost, establishing class differences: First Class, Business Class, Comfort Plus, Main Cabin, and Basic Economy. Each class has carry-on baggage implications.

Major airlines ultimately recognize that all of this conflicts with their need to maintain on-time departures, a published customer service measure, and they generally offer free baggage checking at the gate for passenger volunteers. As passengers, many of us get sucked into the airline perks game, and at the actual moment of boarding, most everyone is still jockeying for position to optimize their chance of getting the coveted overhead compartment space for their roller boards; free baggage checking is a last resort. The functional problem is never addressed, buried beneath the plethora of fragmentation and conflict that will repeat itself over and over.

Without being aware of our innate predisposition to fragment most everything based on our ideals and expectations, we will assemble teams comprised of individuals competing, leveraging, and defending what they value to protect or gain personal advantage. We all have our own best interests as a priority and show up with conflicting opinions, hypotheses, and solutions. We individually focus on what we think *should be* without making an effort to collectively understand what *actually is* going on, the functional problem.

Our persistent focus on our conflicts rather than the functional problem common to everyone disempowers teams from creating new and sustained functional solutions. We have a fragmented and misaligned understanding of the problem. Our solutions are generated from knowledge and experience, which are always an incomplete mixture of facts and ideas. And we unwittingly weave the resulting conflict into our problem-solving approach, which clouds and distracts across multiple levels. The result is, at best, an incremental improvement, more, better, different, and nothing new. No wonder we cringe at the thought of improvement initiatives.

The Approach to Understanding a Problem Is More Important Than the Problem Itself

If we are predisposed to wrapping functional problems in conflict, we are destined to develop and implement partial solutions that perpetuate both. The partial solution becomes the next complication to the functional problem and an additional source of conflict. Surely, there must be a way to escape this endless cycle. It's easy for us to focus on problems and conflict with the notion that the specific solution is most important.

However, we've seen through examples across personal and professional areas that there is a common pattern to problem solving that often leads to suboptimal results, regardless of the problem. The essence of effective problem solving resides in our observation that the *approach to understanding* a problem is more important than the problem itself. What if we could develop a problem-solving methodology that could solve any problem we took on?

WHAT IS TRANSFORMATION?

We can't solve problems using the same thinking that created them to begin with.

—ALBERT EINSTEIN

Our usual approach to problem solving is to apply our knowledge and experience, both of which are retrospective sources of incomplete information, and reshape them into ideal future-state solutions. Essentially, we are trying to create something new from the old. Considering this carefully, our conceived future is a modified continuation of what we're already doing.

I recently bought a Tesla, thinking I would do my small part to reduce carbon emissions and fossil fuel consumption. While I may be improving my immediate surroundings, a detrimental environmental impact is occurring upstream with battery production and increased electrical power plant output, which may be worse. In healthcare, we've spent billions of dollars converting paper-based documentation to the electronic health record. While we may have improved in organizing and coordinating our record-keeping, it has made care documentation much more burdensome for care teams.

If we want to develop authentically new, comprehensive, and sustained solutions, we must move to a problem-solving approach that can create "a thorough or dramatic change in form." This is transformation. In stark contrast to our usual fragmented approach to incremental change, transformation is about seeing problems afresh, comprehensively and without past reference. We must let go of narrowed perspectives, opinions, and assumptions. In essence, transformation is about putting aside what we know and enabling a new mode of understanding to emerge. Our typical next question is "How can we do this?" and as we've said before, we first must understand the why rather than the how.

BREAKING THE CONFLICT CYCLE: MOVING FROM A NULL HYPOTHESIS TO NO HYPOTHESIS

Scientists commonly introduce a theory for solving a research problem in the form of a null hypothesis to reduce the risk of study bias. The null hypothesis is written to propose that the researcher's theory has no meaningful relationship to the problem, and they then try to *disprove* the null hypothesis to show their theory's significance. For example, a researcher might want to test the theory that sunscreen reduces the risk of skin cancer. As part of their study design, their null hypothesis might propose that "the use of sunscreen does not reduce the risk of skin cancer," and they would be looking for their study results to disprove this, thereby supporting their theory that sunscreen does indeed reduce the risk.

In healthcare, we always look for ways to improve patient throughput, which is the length of stay from admission to discharge. One popular theory for increasing early patient discharges is to have providers enter patient discharge orders by 10:00 a.m. The null hypothesis might state, "Provider discharge order entry by 10:00 a.m. does not result in earlier patient discharges." The study would again disprove the null hypothesis if the theory is valid. This evidence-based approach to problem solving has its merits. However, when we look closely at the structure, we can see that we narrowed our scope of inquiry with imposed assumptions, ideas, and possible solutions before we even started exploring. Einstein's quote has already fallen on deaf ears; we're using the old, the known, to create the new.

A radical, and perhaps heretical, leap from incremental to trans-formational problem solving is to shift from a null hypothesis to *no* hypothesis, to start exploring with a blank slate. Instead of creating a null hypothesis for discharge efficiency, what if we started our investigation with an open-ended question regarding identifying *any* issues and concerns related to discharge efficiency? If we start with a null hypothesis, we have limited the scope of our investigation to areas we think are relevant; when we start with no hypothesis, there are no preset boundaries or references.

It can be very unsettling to approach a problem with an "I don't know." However, when we have no hypothesis, we have the freedom to look and to be present as inquisitive learners unencumbered by preconceived opinions, conclusions, and ideas. CLUE Rounding, as I described in chapter 6, is a good example. The freedom to look empowers us to share in open inquiry and active observation, inviting us to see comprehensively what actually is.

For starters, it allows us to uncover the elements of conflict that undermine our ability to fully observe the functional problem we are trying to solve. If we can collectively understand the nature of our fragmentation and conflict, we will usually find a common cause, perhaps seeing for the first time that we are all making similar pointed assumptions about each other being at fault for departure delays. With that awareness, conflict dissolves, and we are left with just the functional fact-based problem. Eliminating conflict creates a safe learning space, enabling us to let go of our opinions further and apply our full attention to comprehensively understanding the functional problem as collaborative learners. We're now all in this together.

What is the source of clarity that emerges from our shift to no hypothesis, the freedom to look, awareness, and understanding to enable transformation?

WHAT IS INSIGHT?

In contrast to incremental problem solving, where we use iterative thinking to develop ideal solutions, transformative problem solving taps insight as a distinct source of immediate clarity and action. Insight is "the capacity to gain an accurate and deep intuitive understanding of something or someone." Where we use thinking to *actively develop* abstract solutions based on prior knowledge and experience, insight generates functional solutions that arise from our comprehensive understanding of the actual problem.

Insight is not the result of willpower or concentration. Rather, it emerges by letting go and enabling observation without direction or motive to occur. Since insight is unrelated to knowledge and experience, it is not thought-dependent and manifests as a sudden flash where everything comes together with clear, correct action. There may be a preceding period of disarray and confusion, but the spontaneous understanding from letting go and observing the whole creates the burst of clarity.

When I was an ENT resident and the anesthesia resident turned to me and said, "It's never too late to change," I instantly understood what I needed to do. When I was in the abyss of isolation and confusion following my adverse event with Linda Kenney, the collapse of my thinking ability unleashed a state of clear, correct action. After three weeks of unfettered observations with the Hospital Medicine service at UAB, I suddenly understood their care model challenges and the path forward. Spontaneous insight catalyzed comprehensive understanding and clarity of action in each of these instances. It's not what you're thinking.

Problem Solving Together: Creating Conditions for Transformation

It is much easier to intellectually describe the distinction between incremental and transformative problem solving than to create actual awareness, understanding, and action. Unless we can move to the latter, we will continue to approach problem solving with fragmentation and conflict. The reality of guiding and supporting change initiatives is that participants inevitably show up to problem solve with partial understanding, opinions, ideas, and preconceived solutions. Participants are not aware of the nature of the fragmentation and conflict that constrain incremental problem solving nor the power of transformation that comes from comprehensive understanding and insight.

You, dear reader, now have the insider's view! To be successful with redesign teams, we have the dual responsibility of creating tangible and effective conditions for developing transformative problem-solving capacity and enabling us to create and implement sustained solutions.

If we establish the correct conditions, our approach to understanding the problem can create a transformative result.

Problem solving together is the secret sauce to transformation, and it is much more than having the right participants on the team roster. As we've already discovered, when we collaborate as a team of open learners, curious and willing to look at our problems comprehensively and objectively, there is no problem that we cannot solve. Enablers of problem solving together include establishing an environment of trust and respect, active team engagement, learning to listen, listening to learn, willingness to explore and let go of opinions, and presenting observations and ideas as inquiry. Disablers are generally those subjective elements that come from fragmentation and conflict, such as maintaining an environment of hierarchy and authority, engaging passive-aggressively, defending opinions, associating opinion change with failure, and presenting ideas and insights as directive.

Enablers:
- Establishing an environment of trust and respect
- Active Engagement (Systems-Based)
- Learning to Listen, Listening to Learn
- Willingness to Explore & Let Go of Opinions
- Presenting Ideas and Insights as Inquiry

Disablers:
- Maintaining an environment of hierarchy and authority
- Passive or Resistant Engagement (Blame)
- Defending Opinions
- Associating Opinion Change with Failure
- Presenting Ideas and Insights as Directive

Most team members have been stuck on the disabled list, and our initial opportunity is to create awareness and restore player functionality and well-being so they can return to active-enabled status.

As coaches, we need an effective methodology that is simple, user-friendly, and accessible to empower and inspire our teams to achieve their full potential. In the next chapter, we will introduce this methodology and explore the engine that brings transformative problem solving to life.

Chapter 8

From Fragmentation to Synergy

Synergy is the only word in our language that means behavior of whole systems unpredicted by the separately observed behaviors of any of the system's separate parts.

—BUCKY FULLER

As we left off in the last chapter, team participants generally show up to improvement initiatives skeptical, stressed, and with fragmented problem-solving approaches that predispose to conflict. We each think we know the problem, have strong ideas of who and what is responsible, and have ideal solutions that would fix the problem if only we were allowed to implement them. Even if we have a leadership role, we often show up in a state of learned helplessness, feeling at risk or disempowered to participate meaningfully in the change process.

We have seen how this recipe prevents us from problem solving together, understanding the functional problem, and creating a trans-formative solution. It is not enough for us to change the problem-solving paradigm with conceptual descriptions and models. It is mostly about action, actively engaging team participants in a way that actualizes the key elements of problem solving together. This chapter will explore the power source that propels our problem-solving methodology toward transformative change.

Precision Problem Solving: Targeted Improvement with Minimal Side Effects

Clay Christensen, the HBS professor who pioneered the field of disruptive innovation, wrote a book titled *The Innovator's Prescription*, in which he coined the term "precision medicine" to describe the treatment of clinical diseases whose causes are completely understood. For the diseases that currently fall into this category, like smallpox and other infectious diseases, Professor Christensen pointed out that a comprehensive understanding of the disease resulted in precise treatments that were curative with minimal to no side effects.[5] Our approach to transforming dysfunctional systems is very similar to precision medicine: understanding the root causes of "diseased" systems completely and creating targeted "curative" solutions that are functional and sustained with minimal side effects. Out of this observation, we named our methodology "Precision Problem Solving."

---

5   C. M. Christensen, J. Grossman, and J. Hwang, *The Innovator's Prescription* (McGraw Hill, 2009), 46.

PRECISION PROBLEM SOLVING

The implementation of solutions for systems challenges that can be precisely diagnosed, whose causes are understood, and which consequently can be transformed with evidence-based interventions that are predictably effective.

How does Precision Problem Solving (PrecisionPS) provide a simple, user-friendly, and accessible approach to creating conditions for transformative change? As we observed earlier, one of the core tenets of PrecisionPS is that the *approach* to understanding a problem is more important than the problem itself. To that end, our goal in creating the PrecisionPS methodology is to be able to use it to solve *any* problem.

To Move beyond Fragmentation and Conflict, We Have to See It

(Mis)Perception

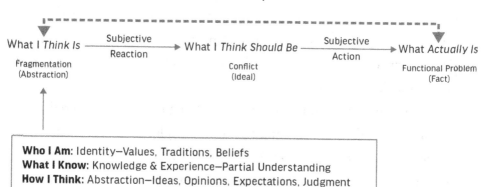

Recall that our perception of what *is,* the functional problem, is immediately fragmented by who I am, what I know, and how I think. We are really misperceiving what *is* based on our subjective filters for seeing the problem. When we experience a contradiction between what we think *is* and our subjective mosaic of what we think *should be*, we react in conflict.

We've observed how our problem-solving efforts immediately center on resolving our conflict and the associated symptoms of stress. It's miserable to feel frustrated, fatigued, and trapped. We want out, but here's the rub: we mistakenly attribute the source of our conflict to the outer functional problem rather than our inner fragmentation. Facts (what *actually is*) are never in conflict. It's our subjective interpretation of the facts (what we *think is*) compared to our ideals (what we *think should be*) that creates conflict.

We try to resolve our conflict by solving the objective problem with the same subjective approach that is causing our conflict to begin with. The insanity of this is we're trying to solve conflict with conflict! When we try to use ideals to solve problems without understanding the facts, neither the functional problem nor our conflict gets transformed. Since we don't see the source of our conflict, we don't get to the source of the functional problem either. Instead, we get caught in a perpetual loop of cause and effect where our conflict complicates the functional problem, exacerbating our conflict and further complicating the functional problem. And around we go. We're increasingly stressed, and the complexity we've created largely obscures the core issues.

One of the common frustrations I regularly encountered as a surgical resident was getting lab tests completed on time for my patients. For multiple reasons beyond my grasp, it would take hours to get lab results back to inform clinical decision-making, time that I did not have in my demanding schedule. I found the lack of efficient service unacceptable, and I needed a solution to relieve my stress and expedite lab turnaround.

I resorted to ordering my labs STAT, misusing an order designation intended for patients requiring urgent or emergent results. This occasionally achieved my intended result, but most of the time, it did not, because ordering STAT labs had become common among most residents. Our increasing use of STAT labs routinized the order designation. It eliminated its intended value such that we now had to personally draw the blood and hand-deliver the samples to the lab for testing for our critically ill patients with an actual urgent need for labs. The result: greater process complexity with no functional improvement, greater frustration with no resolution of conflict, and a decline in care quality and patient safety. Again, we can't solve conflict with conflict; we can't solve functional problems with ideals.

Harnessing the Power of Synergy

Think about how difficult and even threatening it would be to introduce the Fragmentation-Conflict Cycle to a newly formed improvement team. It would likely be a kickoff in conflict. We've seen how important relationship building is in establishing a safe learning environment. To that end, we have an engine that reliably empowers and supports precision problem-solving teams as transformation initiatives progress.

There are three sets of principles we harness as the power source of PrecisionPS: Systems Principles, Participatory Management Principles, and Peer Support Principles. While the first two sets of principles are well described and applied in other improvement approaches, we often use them in isolation or in fragments. The power of Precision

Problem Solving resides in the integration of the three. When this triad of principles is combined, their strength is synergistic or greater than the sum of their parts, like steel made of iron, carbon, and alloy metal. We can start to see that Precision Problem Solving is about taking an integrated holistic approach to eliminating fragmentation and conflict so that teams can place full attention on solving the functional problem.

We can't understand fragmentation and conflict using the same approach that created it; thank you, Einstein! Essentially, we're saying that we must understand the systems interrelationships between organizations, teams, and individuals to dissolve conflict and solve functional problems. Let's explore how the Precision Problem Solving engine runs.

Systems Principles: To see the fragmentation of systems and their interrelationships, we need to understand systems structure and function.

Purpose, Elements, and Interconnections: When we try to understand complex structures, we usually break them down into manageable components, which we classify as systems. In *Thinking in Systems*, Donella Meadows describes a system as "an interconnected set of elements that is coherently organized in a way that achieves something."[6] Systems consist of a defined purpose, functional elements, and interconnections between the elements and their surroundings.

For example, within professional sports, the National Football League is an organizational system that aims to enable football

---

6   Donella H. Meadows, *Thinking in Systems—A Primer* (White River Junction: Chelsea Green Publishing, 2008).

teams to compete and for the best team to ultimately become the season's Super Bowl champion. To enable the competition, the NFL comprises elements including teams, referees, public spectators, and stadiums, which interconnect through league regulations, game rules, and personal interaction. A football team, such as the Cleveland Browns, is an NFL subsystem that aims to win football games and the Super Bowl championship with players and coaches using offensive, defensive, and special teams when they play other teams.

A football player is a subsystem within a team. Their purpose is to be the best at their position and to do their job so that the team wins games and becomes the Super Bowl champion. Players are expected to be physically fit, mentally prepared, and experts in understanding and executing their functional roles and responsibilities. Who they are, what they know, and how they think determine their interconnections within the team and the league. Sound familiar?

Healthcare organizations aspire to provide high-quality, safe, and efficient care and support clinical specialties like cardiology with complex elements like hospital administration, clinical departments, nursing, ancillary services, and well-equipped care areas such as cath labs and critical care units. Interconnections holding the system together include regulatory standards, policies and guidelines, scheduling, and care coordination. A division of cardiology is a healthcare subsystem whose purpose might be to deliver exceptional cardiac care with the mantra of "Right Patient, Right Care, Right Setting, Right Time."

System elements include physicians and nurse practitioners, division leadership, administration, patients, and families. There are numerous interconnections such as cardiology board certification, payor guidelines, division policies, and collaborative care with other services. Like the NFL football player, the cardiologist is an individual subsystem within the cardiology division with a very similar purpose related to being the best, doing their job, and elevating their division to top-tier status. Cardiologists are expected to be critical thinkers and experts in understanding and executing their functional roles and responsibilities. Who they are, what they know, and how they think also determine their interconnections within the team and the organization. Notice how, at the individual system level, there is a system convergence regardless of profession. Awareness of this common denominator is important!

We can appreciate in both examples how systems and subsystems fragment simultaneously while expanding interconnections to each other. Achieving the intended results is complicated, even in the best circumstances. The more knowledge and experience we acquire about our systems, the more sophisticated they become and the more fragmented we tend to make them. It becomes increasingly difficult for us to stay on top of the additional complexity, so we subspecialize further. In football, we have players who function exclusively on special teams, such as kickoff returns; in cardiology, we have subspecialty physicians who focus on heart failure or advanced cardiac imaging.

As we continue to develop our concentrated expertise, the systems trap we unwittingly fall into is losing sight of our connection to the big picture and the integrated whole. The complexity and fragmentation of the systems and subsystems we create become unmanageable, particularly when we lose sight of our collective purpose and get caught in the tangled web of interconnections. We begin to feel like the systems are controlling us rather than the other way around; we're working for the system rather than the system working for us. Now we're in conflict, our familiar companion, and we begin to search for relief or escape from our distress, often to the further detriment of our personal well-being.

In the NFL, an athlete's fundamental passion for playing football may be overshadowed by the pressure to win, attain celebrity status, and score a mega-million-dollar contract. In academic medicine, the physician's passion for treating patients may be overshadowed by the pressure of productivity targets, achieving academic promotion, and being awarded multimillion-dollar research grants. In both cases, we've lost our sense of direction and think that achieving these tangential objectives will make us better and restore our well-being, only to find that it adds additional stress and questions like, What if we don't win, don't achieve fame, and don't win the lottery? Our passion for the game and our joy in work have evaporated.

Although a minority of participants successfully maneuver in the system's morass, they remain trapped within the ambiguous system boundaries like the others. Our aligned purpose and ability to see the functional whole has been lost, and we tend to become very protective and defensive of what we can control. Inevitably, we focus on what we think works best for us individually, which begins to suboptimize the interconnected system elements and outputs with unintended consequences: celebrity status and massive contract disparities create resentment and isolation, which compromises team cohesiveness; the team begins to lose, and revenue begins to drop as fan support and media coverage decline; coaches get fired; and teams get sold and relocate to rebuild. And around we go again. We can't resolve conflict with conflict.

Core Systems Principles: Systems principles help us introduce and solidify the foundations of systems structure and function for improvement teams since most of us construct and participate in systems without full awareness. As a counterpoint to our general use of systems to simplify and organize complex structures into separate functional subcomponents, systems principles emphasize the interconnectedness and the holistic behavior of the parts. Systems principles remind us that everything is connected and that what happens in one system will impact everything else. For example, in 1982, the NFL players went on strike with financial demands and shut down the entire NFL for seven regular season games, impacting the entire organization from the NFL leadership and team owners to the spectators. Everything is connected.

We incorporate several systems principles into PrecisionPS such as the Perfectly Designed Rule, based on Paul Bataldan's observation that every system is perfectly designed to deliver the result it gets.[7] This principle points out that there are no systems mistakes, just unintended consequences. It also highlights the breadth of systems interconnectedness and our collective accountability for the functional results we get. Most of us tend to think of systems as mechanical or operational structures within which we interact. However, our football and healthcare examples reveal how teams and individuals are influential subsystems that contribute to outcomes, good or bad. In the NFL, think about the ripple effect of the goal of winning the Super Bowl financially: enormous revenue gains for the league through media coverage, revenue incentives to teams for winning, and player demands for a significant share of that revenue (especially if they have exceptional talent). This was part of the reason for the 1982 players' strike. The system is perfectly designed to do this. In seeing our collective responsibility for what is going on, we emphasize the opportunity for us to affect change where we might have thought not previously possible.

---

7   Susan Carr, "A Quotation with a Life of Its Own," Editor's Notebook, Patient Safety and Quality Healthcare, 2008, https://www.psqh.com/analysis/editor-s-notebook-a-quotation-with-a-life-of-its-own/.

A second principle we introduce is W. Edwards Deming's 94% Rule, which states that at least 94 percent of outcomes, good or bad, result from complex systems, with only 6 percent or less resulting from individual effort.[8] This principle emphasizes that, while individuals are part of the structure and function of complex systems, comprehensive systems improvement is more effective than individual improvement. Without a high-functioning offensive line, a talented quarterback will be constrained and have limited success in winning games. Similarly, a talented cardiologist subspecialized in advanced cardiac imaging will have limited impact if the imaging equipment is not well maintained or unavailable. Perhaps one of the most important takeaways from the 94% Rule for improvement teams is that we should not immediately assign individual blame for unintended outcomes. Recall how easy and ingrained this behavior was when I had my adverse event with Linda. Rather than assigning blame and shame, we create an opening for understanding and root-cause problem solving.

The third fundamental principle we incorporate is the Critical 20% Rule or Pareto's Law, which states that approximately 20 percent of the system variables create 80 percent of the results.[9] For example, a football team likely runs 20 percent of its plays 80 percent of the time. In cardiology, 20 percent of heart failure patients might comprise 80 percent of heart failure patients admitted to hospitals. We apply this principle to underscore the importance of consistently targeting the Critical 20% areas that give us the biggest improvement bang for our buck. There are so many moving parts and interconnections in complex systems that it is easy to get overwhelmed, sidetracked, and go down rabbit holes.

---

8   W. Edwards Deming, *Out of the Crisis* (Cambridge: The MIT Press, 2000), 270.

9   Vilfredo Pareto, *Cours d'conomie Politique, Volume I and II* (Lausanne: F. Rouge, 1896, 1897).

Combined with our two prior rules, we take the time and effort to understand the systems to guide us to the Critical 20% rather than making assumptions and jumping to solutions. For example, heart failure patients admitted to a cardiology service might have long hospital lengths of stay. Rather than assume that we should focus on the sickest patients with the longest length of stay, our systems assessment might reveal that there is more improvement opportunity in optimizing the care progression of the *less* sick patients because they get less immediate attention from the care teams; perhaps only 20 percent of patients get 80 percent of the cardiologist's attention. As we will see later, we also leverage participant conflict and stress to effectively target Critical 20% improvement areas in understanding systems.

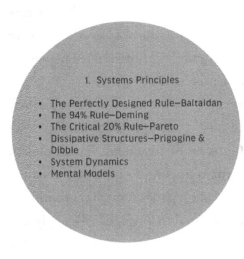

Relevance

1. Systems Principles

- The Perfectly Designed Rule—Baltaldan
- The 94% Rule—Deming
- The Critical 20% Rule—Pareto
- Dissipative Structures—Prigogine & Dibble
- System Dynamics
- Mental Models

- No mistakes, Everything Connected, Collective Accountability
- Collective System Function Dominates Individual Effort, Focus on Systems Not People
- Identify and Understand the Critical Areas for Maximum Value and Impact
- Threshold Resistance to Change
- System Integration, Complexity and Feedback Loops, Leverage Points
- Perception and Reality vs. Observation and Actuality

We embed additional systems principles and disciplines into PrecisionPS to reinforce the importance of systems integration and complexity and the breadth of their existence from the collective down to the level of individual thought in the form of our mental models. As we have observed in our recent systems examples, individual purpose and interconnections converge around who I am, what I know, and how I think. Understanding participatory management principles as the next engine component of Precision Problem Solving pulls us closer to this.

Participatory Management Principles: To understand how systems structure and function in achieving our goals and well-being, we must engage and empower participants to openly share their diverse perspectives and expertise.

Purpose and Interconnections: As we have seen in complex systems, fragmentation predisposes us to lose clarity of purpose and understanding of the vast internal and external interconnections. Complex systems have so many moving parts that it is easier for us to operate them autonomously. Coaches want to manage their teams without owner involvement; nurses want to care for their patients rather than spend hours documenting care in the electronic health record.

We specialize and develop expertise in subsystems, and before we know it, we have built silos that strain interconnections and reduce situational awareness. We naturally establish leadership roles at the highest systems levels with a cascade of leaders and managers down to the front lines. Given the scope of responsibility, it becomes very easy for senior leaders to lose direct touch with the front lines and become dependent on information their subordinates relay. Inevitably, this information is incomplete and delayed, which often creates conflict and a reactive urgency to "do something."

Without fully seeing and understanding the functional problems, leaders often assume a reactive "firefighting" posture and put out the visible fire with a quick fix by jumping to a solution. A good example of this was when I was a surgical intern and hospital administration removed all the unapproved finger-stick blood glucose monitors off of the patient floors in preparation for a hospital accreditation visit by the Joint Commission. We clinicians were left having to personally draw multiple daily patient blood samples and take them to the lab until the weeklong visit was over. Since firefighting is an everyday occurrence, the ability to respond quickly and decisively to problems is a highly valued, if not required, attribute of strong leadership. While these are essential leadership capabilities, the slippery slope emerges when firefighting becomes equated with systems improvement.

Leaders are susceptible to pushing preconceived and partially formed solutions to the recipient front lines for rapid implementation when this occurs. Frontline teams may be asked to weigh in on the proposed solutions. However, the conversation is often more of a leadership focus group or sales pitch for buying into their plan rather than a codevelopment opportunity. In the absence of frontline expertise, even well-intended proposed solutions are usually misaligned and oversimplified, focusing on the visible manifestations of the problem rather than the root cause. We may put out the flames, but we don't extinguish the embers. The likely result is more fragmentation, conflict, and limited improvement. The attempt to manage the cost of OR scrubs with automated dispensing units when I was an anesthesia resident is a good example of a misaligned top-down driven leadership initiative that failed; it nevertheless offered a moment of levity when the frustrated anesthesiology attending walked into the OR in his boxer shorts!

Participatory management principles are important for actively engaging multidisciplinary frontline teams in problem solving as part of the functional PrecisionPS framework. Drawing on our understanding of the fragmentation-conflict cycle and the systems principles we previously described, we can appreciate that everyone involved in a complex system and their subsystems possesses different perspectives and areas of expertise. If we are going to be able to understand a complex system comprehensively, we need to recognize and leverage these varied inputs. Recall the value and importance of open inquiry and having no hypothesis when we investigate a problem fully. We must enable diverse team representation and create a safe learning environment that empowers everyone to share their functional expertise with the rest of the team.

Deference to Expertise: It can be particularly challenging for leaders to embrace active frontline engagement and defer to their diverse expertise in a cultural setting that values quick and decisive action. Leaders may worry about losing control and be concerned that frontline-driven problem solving will result in a chaotic free-for-all. Similarly, frontline team members may feel insubordinate and fear retribution if they challenge leaders or professionals with presumed elevated status. A player can't challenge a coach, and a nurse can't challenge a physician, right? Notice the conflict. It is therefore important to point out to improvement teams that deference to expertise is functional and not hierarchical.

Functional expertise occurs at every level and in every subsystem of an organization, and we need to leverage this as much as possible when we problem solve. Senior leaders have functional expertise in guiding and supporting organizational strategic planning, finance, and operations. In that capacity, leaders serve a critical role in defining the why and the what in problem solving. Multidisciplinary frontline team members have functional expertise in providing the actual outputs and services, and they play a key part in designing and implementing the how in alignment with the why and the what.

For example, let's say hospital leadership identifies a patient safety issue that points to an improvement need in activating care for patients arriving at the emergency department with chest pain. Leadership empowers a multiprofessional frontline team of care professionals and support staff to leverage their functional expertise in care delivery to understand the problem and develop a sustainable solution based on the Critical 20% opportunities identified. Leadership uses their expertise to define the why and what and defers to frontline expertise to determine the how. Importantly, leadership remains actively engaged with the team, using their expertise to guide and support the advancement of the initiative and mitigating barriers.

Let's look at how framing roles and responsibilities in terms of functional expertise rather than hierarchy creates conditions for a safe learning environment. When we recognize that multiprofessional team members have distinct areas of expertise, it becomes possible for us to appreciate our own knowledge strengths and gaps; we develop an awareness of the value that full team engagement brings in seeing the whole problem. This awareness opens us to say, "I don't know, but collectively we do." We begin to let go of our subjective opinions and the pressure of knowing it all and objectively listen to the expertise of others.

The subjective conditions that predispose to hierarchy start to dissolve, which enables team members to function objectively on a level playing field—coaches and players bring their functional expertise from the stadium, physicians and nurses bring their expertise from the patient care unit, and no one is more important than the other. We can now tap into the group's collective genius to understand and solve the functional problem. When we are empowered to problem solve together, we create team ownership around a common purpose: the solution we ultimately implement is ours.

Relevance

- Awareness that perceptions are fragmented and limit ability to see what's actually happening (situational awareness)
- Appreciation of different perspectives pulls people out of silos to see commonalities
- Creating a safe learning environment
- Being comfortable with "I don't know"
- Clear leadership responsibilities for guidance and support to promote collective accountability
- Embracing functional expertise (leveling the playing field)
- The "collective genius" of the team can solve most problems when understood
- Engagement and empowerment

2. Participatory Management Principles

- Recognizing and Leveraging Varied Perspectives
- Deference to Expertise
- Shared Decision-Making with Frontline Staff
- Ownership vs. Buy-In
- Standard Work for Leaders

We have seen how participatory management principles form an integrated link to systems principles, strengthening system interconnections between the multidisciplinary teams, the structural elements, and their aligned purpose. Organizational systems are interconnected with team systems through both sets of principles, each influencing and reinforcing the other. The success of its football teams primarily determines the success of the NFL, and vice versa; the success of a healthcare system is largely determined by the success of its clinical departments, and vice versa.

The common element of organizational and team systems is the individual, the personal system driven by who I am, what I know, and how I think. We now need to understand how individuals relate to organizational and team systems. Since we all experience conflict as individuals, and it strongly influences our actions, peer support principles are the keystone to addressing this and creating a sustainable, safe learning environment as the third PrecisionPS engine component.

> Peer Support Principles: To enable participants to openly share their diverse perspectives and expertise with each other, we need to create a safe learning environment that eliminates conflict.

The Relationship between Fragmentation, Conflict, and Change: We are all aware that problem solving involves change and that change can be very stressful. A well-known phrase states, "The magnitude of change is proportional to the emotional intensity of the experience." If I have to change shampoos because of scalp irritation, it's not that big a deal. If I have a death in the family, that has a significant impact. Small change, minimal emotion; big change, high emotion.

Interestingly, my emotional response to change can be very different from another's response to the same scenario. For example, my wife might be distraught over having to switch shampoos; she has a full head of beautiful hair, and I am bald! This would be the same *functional* change but with much higher emotional intensity. Perhaps there is more to the magnitude of change than meets the eye. Let's see if we can understand why these distinctions show up and how this might connect to fragmentation and conflict.

I'm always amazed at how word definitions reveal nuances in their interpretation and use. In the dictionary, "change" is defined in two contexts: one related to *objective* or functional change and the other to *subjective* or personal change. Appreciate the difference: objective, to *make* different, alter, or modify; and subjective, to *be* different, to *be* altered or modified. As we saw with a change in shampoo, the emotional response to change depends on how much it affects us personally.

Here's another example: If an airline changes its frequent flier program where it is now more difficult for us to reach benefit levels, it results in different passenger responses. An infrequent traveler may be completely indifferent to the change, a frequent flier who now has the bar raised to reach their target level may be very upset, and the road warrior may be glad that their easily achieved elite status is now more exclusive because now there will be no more lines to get into the airline lounges.

Functional change made *organizationally* is quite variable in how it affects us personally. We don't have to *be* different. On the other hand, if we have to change how we function at work, like having to relinquish our autonomous clinical practice for a more standardized team approach, or we develop a clinical condition, like diabetes, where we have to make significant lifestyle changes, these changes are progressively personal, strong, and consistent, which can create a lot of stress. We have much less ability to opt out, and the change becomes increasingly personal; we have to *be* different, the ones who have to change. Notice how closely personal change is related to stress and conflict.

These examples show us that our perceived magnitude of change has much more to do with personal impact than structural size. The greater the personal change required in a system redesign, the greater our personal conflict in making those changes. Additionally, the greater the system redesign, the greater the number of people who also will be personally impacted. So, the challenge of scope and size in systems change is related to how much the change and the number of people involved personally impact us. Watch how our discovery brings us back to a common source: the greater the systems change, the greater the number of people impacted by *personal* change; the greater the *personal* change, the greater the *personal* conflict; and the greater the *personal* conflict, the greater the *personal* fragmentation—who I am, what I know, and how I think. Since personal fragmentation and conflict are connected to individual change, and individuals are connected to teams and organizations, problem solving has to address personal conflict for change to be transformative across all system levels.

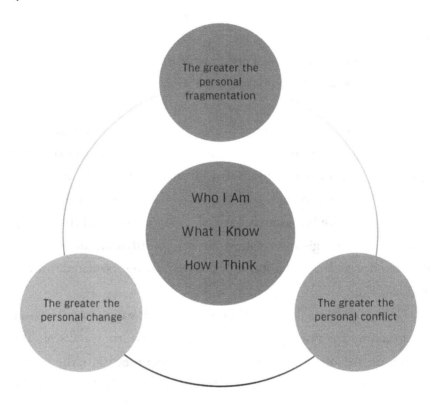

As I shared with you in chapter 4, the medical catastrophe I experienced with Linda Kenney was the most stressful event of my life. The event's aftermath in the following weeks aligns very closely with the model we just described. The initial shock spun my head in a whirlwind of fragmented thought, questioning how I could have done this to Linda, looking at the nerve block process from all angles to find where I had gone wrong, getting more stressed and conflicted the more I dissected the event. My life changed instantly with the loss of self-confidence, isolation, and shame. Because I had nowhere to go to decompress my distress, my breakthrough came from a thought implosion that inexplicably created a flash of insight. The clarity from the insight became the catalyst for transformative personal change, which led me to create a peer support program for my perioperative team that then expanded to the health system level. It started with *being* the change with Linda and translated to our *making* the expanded change happen.

Most change events will not be that intense, thank goodness, but there are plenty of complex problem-solving scenarios where conflict brings teams very close to collapse. Rather than ignoring conflict associated with problem solving and change or driving participants over an emotional cliff with the hope that an insight parachute will prevent a crash landing, applying peer support principles is an effective way for us to decompress conflict, enhance wellness, and reinforce conditions for a safe learning environment.

Connecting as Colleagues: Peer support principles enable us to focus attention on individual stressors, creating opportunities for team members to share and reflect on their issues and concerns on how they relate to each other and their environment. It's important to remember that the term "peer" indicates that we offer support from one colleague to another and that we understand each other as team members. This means that we as facilitators must have similar professional backgrounds and experiences connecting us to what team members share. For example, if we were problem solving with an NFL team, we would have facilitator peers with NFL experience matching the team participants, such as players and coaches. We have the same alignment in healthcare settings, ensuring we have physician and nursing peer facilitators. As facilitators, we start out as peers supporting the team members, and ultimately, our goal is to enable and empower team members to support each other in a peer setting.

Attentive Listening: One of the most difficult things for us is to give someone our undivided attention. Consider how many different thoughts go through our minds as we go about our day or when speaking with someone. Chances are that we're in a constant state of analytic comparison, assessing how the other is behaving, examining whether we agree with what they're saying, and thinking about how we want to respond before they finish. In other words, we're really not paying attention or listening to them as much as we're judging how they align with what we value.

Attentive listening is a core principle of peer support that allows participants to share issues, concerns, and ideas with actual contact. Unlike concentration, which requires intentional effort to focus on what's being said while blocking out distractions, attentive listening is unprompted and begins with our awareness that we are *not* paying attention. In seeing our distractions, attentive listening innately emerges.

Attentive listening puts us in a space of being fully present for the other participants, inviting them to share without our generating opinions, judgment, or expectations. In many cases, this is the first time participants' voices are heard, and it can be equally novel for us as teammates to be listening. For example, if we're trying to understand the causes of hospital discharge delays, clinicians learn a great deal from their environmental services colleagues when they share their challenges of having to prioritize and coordinate room cleaning for multiple simultaneous requests; we're all so caught up in our specialty domains that we lack situational awareness. As participants share and listen, the environment for open inquiry and collaborative learning is reinforced. We're collectively expanding our awareness rather than reinforcing and defending boundaries. This environment is further solidified with the presence of a second inherent core peer support principle: compassion.

Compassion: Compassion is a term commonly confused with sympathy and empathy. Whereas the latter two express our understanding or emotional connection to someone else's suffering, compassion expands these expressions to include corrective action. Using an oversimplified analogy, if someone is suffering with a thorn in their foot, a sympathetic person understands their suffering, an empathetic person feels their suffering, and a compassionate person understands or feels their suffering and helps them remove the thorn.

While compassion is action-oriented, like attentive listening, it is neither deliberate nor selective. The opening for compassion emerges when we become aware that our concerns, passions, and outreach to connect with others are selective and primarily based on what we value (sound familiar?). For example, we may be more inclined to support international hunger relief programs than local food banks. In healthcare, we may feel more sympathy for the cardiac patient who lives a "healthy" life than one who has a long-standing history of substance abuse. Becoming aware that our comparative fragmentation is not compassion becomes our opportunity for change. Like attentive listening, compassion acts without opinion, judgment, or expectation. The unspoken message that compassion conveys is, "We care," which empowers team members to acknowledge and support each other, openly share sources of conflict, and appreciate the common connection that everyone has to each other and the problem being addressed.

We can see how the combination of attentive listening and compassion synergize in optimizing conditions for collaborative change. When we create conditions where we actually listen to each other in a caring, nonjudgmental manner, we build trusting relationships.

Mutual trust empowers us to share openly and enhances our appreciation of other perspectives, which in turn contributes to creating a safe learning environment. The actions that emerge from these peer support principles are both passive and active. Compassionate listening creates an inner space for us to reflect on our own issues and concerns as well as those of our teammates and to see common connections. It also inspires us to assume collective responsibility for making active system changes that benefit everyone. The combination of the two contributes to restoring team wellness in the immediate and long-term team setting.

Relevance

3. Peer Support Principles

- Acknowledge and Support Emotional Distress
- Collegial Credibility
- Attentive Listening (No Hypothesis)
- Compassion

- Understand the importance of qualitative data
- Appreciate the presence and role of conflict
- Establish equitable connections
- Build relationships and trust
- Elicit targeted system sources of stressors
- Create conditions for psychological safety
- Create conditions that support wellness

The Synergy of the PrecisionPS Principles: Putting It All Together

As we mentioned at the beginning of the chapter, it is very common for us to apply guiding principles selectively and superficially in our problem-solving approaches, which often lead to limited and unsustainable results. We are also prone to fragmenting the guiding principles into specific areas. For example, we might limit the application of systems principles to structural or technical challenges at the organizational level, such as increasing hospital bed capacity to solve overcrowding without engaging teams to improve care process efficiency. We might only apply participatory management principles to enhance team engagement, such as providing leadership training for managers and directors without practical problem-solving skills. Peer support principles might only be applied to individual clinicians in the form of emotional support programs following adverse clinical events.

The power of Precision Problem Solving resides in our understanding that all three sets of guiding principles apply concurrently at *all systems levels*. We have shown how the simultaneous application of systems, participatory management, and peer support principles creates synergies for complex organizational problem solving. We understand how structure and function achieve an integrated organizational output, we actively engage multidisciplinary teams on a level playing field to harness their collective genius, and we emotionally support team members to create a safe learning environment that eliminates conflict and enables change. We have also discovered that team and individual problem solving require us to apply the same synergistic power principles to create conditions for sustained transformation. Like organizations, teams and individuals are integrated systems with diverse expertise and experience that we need to engage, understand, and empower in a safe learning environment.

Notice the telescopic relationship between these system levels: organizations are comprised of teams, and teams are made up of individuals. In order to solve organizational problems, we have to solve team and individual problems simultaneously. We as individuals are the common systems element throughout, and as our numbers increase at each successive systems level, the complexity of our problems, fragmentation, and conflict also balloon. We may have less individual ability to impact systems outputs as they grow in size and complexity, but organizational and team transformation depend on our individual transformation. Everything is connected, and by harnessing the powerful synergy of systems, participatory management, and peer support principles, our PrecisionPS methodology has the generator to create conditions for comprehensive transformation.

In the next section, we will share how we use Precision Problem Solving as a simple, user-friendly, and accessible methodology to move from chaos to the Critical 20%.

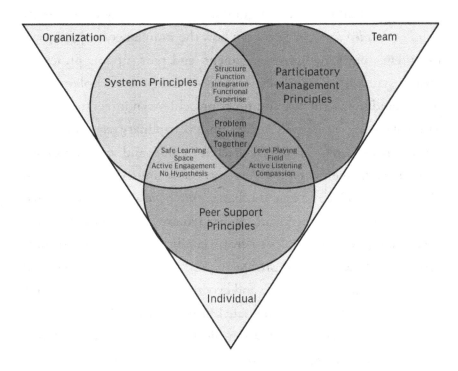

SECTION III

Understanding to Act

Chapter 9

3D Prioritization: From Null to No Hypothesis

We do not think and talk about what we see; we see what we are able to think and talk about.

—EDGAR SCHEIN

We are aware of the significant challenges we face in our personal and professional lives and how they extend outwardly into society. Healthcare is no exception, and for all of the attention we have placed on solving the complex challenges related to quality, safety, and performance, many organizational leaders recognize that profound and urgent change is needed. We had a recent strategic planning retreat at my organization, where an outside strategic consultant shared some sobering statistics regarding the successful implementation of change and strategy: approximately 70 percent of change initiatives fail, with only 43 percent of employees willing to participate in the change;

and approximately 67 percent of strategic plans fail, with 85 percent of leadership teams only spending one hour or less per month on strategic planning.

Their takeaway message: change is hard, we don't spend enough proactive time on long-term objectives, and execution is critical to sustained success. These findings affirm the unsuccessful improvement efforts that we have all experienced in our travails and are a testament to our ongoing attempt to use the same problem-solving approaches that got us where we are to begin with. We're not learning anything new and are still on the path of improvement, which is more, better, and different. If we are going to transform healthcare, and anything else for that matter, we must approach problem solving with fresh eyes.

We are inherently resistant to change, and there are theories that we are hardwired for survival such that in an uncertain environment, we seek security by clinging to what we know. While this no doubt has validity, the opportunity for transformation resides in our understanding that what we *know*, our accumulated knowledge, is a convoluted mix of facts and ideas, distorting our perception of what's happening. Perhaps we are confusing our functional physiological hardwiring for survival with our subjective cultural conditioning for security.

Many instances demonstrate the power of dispelling the latter. For example, job security is considered essential for ensuring the fundamental survival elements of food, shelter, and clothing. In 2020, the COVID-19 pandemic created tremendous employment disruption, including working remotely from home and job losses. The amount of personal change was profound, and in dealing directly with this hardship, many recognized that their job insecurity, showing up in the form of new working conditions or alternate jobs, actually realigned their functional needs to an enhanced lifestyle, and they didn't go back. Their "hardwiring" for our ideal of job security was actually a malleable mindset, which, when recognized, enabled them to shift from "survive" to "thrive." When we create conditions with Precision Problem Solving that enable us to dispel the notion that resistance to change is hardwired by understanding that much of our resistance is actually due to pliable conditioning, such as traditions and assumptions, we can move well beyond the constraints of conventional improvement approaches.

There are multiple problem-solving methodologies out there, from the familiar, like Lean and Six Sigma, to the less common, such as Kaizen and Design Thinking. All of them have specific focus areas as well as common process elements. For example, Lean focuses on reducing waste, Six Sigma is about reducing defects, Kaizen emphasizes continuous improvement with small incremental change, and Design Thinking leverages empathy to identify problems to ideate potential solutions. All of these methodologies use forms of brainstorming to capture multiple inputs and identify improvement opportunities.

While these improvement methodologies offer incremental value, we can readily observe that every one of them is insular and will not create conditions for comprehensive understanding and sustained solutions to complex problems. When we investigate whether the triad set of principles that work synergistically in Precision Problem Solving are used in these methodologies, we observe that the synergy is absent. Lean, Six Sigma, and Kaizen overlook the qualitative issues addressed by the peer support principles, and Design Thinking largely overlooks systems principles by jumping to ideated solutions. As the Meatloaf song goes, "Two out of three ain't bad," but this won't create transformative outcomes. If we observe carefully, there is also a lapse in addressing the role that conflict plays in solving problems; we're generating fragmented solutions based on *what we think should be* (ideas) rather than *what actually is* (facts). This is not to disparage existing improvement methodologies but to underscore the need for a new improvement paradigm that pulls us way beyond the current 30 percent success rate for sustainable change.

We have learned in the preceding chapters that the magnitude and complexity of daily challenges result from their reinforcing circular interplay of fragmentation, conflict, and underlying functional problems. We're aware of how this influences our ability to change, and we've observed how the triad of systems, participatory management, and peer support principles work in synergy to power Precision Problem Solving to create new conditions for transformation. We now have to apply this understanding to act.

Keep It Simple, User-Friendly, and Accessible

I have learned the hard way that if we use a complex and unwieldy improvement methodology with a team inherently resistant to change, we are setting ourselves up to fail. Although we spend most of our lives problem solving, it sits in the backdrop to our prioritized activities, and we don't want it to surface as additional effort or distraction. For example, when a busy clinician is asked to participate in an improvement initiative, it's not uncommon for them to say, "I'm here to take care of my patients and don't have time for meetings and side projects." At home, think about how we use and complain about dull kitchen knives for cooking rather than trying to sharpen them. We say, "I'm too busy, I don't have a sharpener, and sharpeners don't work anyway." Some attribute this attitude to laziness, but if we look closely, we see that we're all very busy and don't have the bandwidth to add another activity that we perceive to have little value. If we're going to be successful in engaging people in meaningful change, we have to use a methodology that is simple, user-friendly, and accessible.

Precision Problem Solving is comprised of three phases that address relevant questions for teams experiencing complex challenges: 3D Prioritization, which defines what matters most to them; Understand and Solve, which gets to the root of what's actually happening to develop a targeted and functional solution; and Launch with Continuous Improvement, which creates relevant and sustained outcomes. While many quality improvement leaders assert that conventional methodologies are like PrecisionPS, our emphasis on facilitating frontline teams in understanding and solving what matters most to *them,* beginning with 3D Prioritization, is what piques frontline attention and gets them to see our methodology as distinct from other improvement approaches.

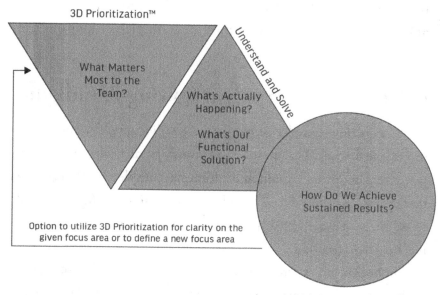

3D Prioritization—Moving from Conflict to the Critical 20%

We've seen in previous chapters how we are generally set up to be ineffective problem solvers, particularly when we come together as teams trying to create mutually beneficial solutions. To solve functional problems, we must create the capability and capacity for problem solving together. 3D Prioritization is a facilitated team exercise designed around several core objectives, enabling us to begin problem solving together and identify the critical pain points from which to prioritize our transformation efforts. These core objectives include creating a safe learning environment, exposing our collective fragmentation and conflict that obscure the ingrained functional problem, seeing that the recognized core functional problem can be collaboratively solved, and becoming an integrated improvement team. For 3D Prioritization to succeed, we must carefully prepare for game time.

Reframing the Problem-Solving Paradigm

We've seen how our desire to resolve conflict quickly, particularly in volatile settings like personal relationships or healthcare delivery, generates suboptimal results and additional complexity. 3D Prioritization creates the space for us to pull ourselves out of firefighting mode, to pause, take a deep breath, and look at what's going on rather than mechanically reacting.

In healthcare, where urgent responses are an everyday occurrence, we have to enable teams to slow down and clarify and leverage the strengths that leaders and frontline members possess. We must ensure that leaders understand the objectives of Precision Problem Solving and 3D Prioritization and that they are committed and accountable to serving as active team sponsors who defer to frontline expertise, mitigate barriers, and support implementation. Similarly, we must enable frontline team members to apply their functional expertise in understanding and transforming their clinical systems and processes in alignment with strategic imperatives. Finally, we have to underscore that 3D Prioritization is an exploration with no preset assumptions or hypotheses, which may reveal unanticipated critical systems interconnections that could become part of the subsequent PrecisionPS initiative. In other words, we follow the breadcrumb trails to their source.

SELECTING THE PLAYERS

We know that complex systems problems are typically comprised of misaligned processes fastidiously held together by the well-intended efforts of the expert end users. We set up 3D Prioritization to uncover the systems fragmentation and their relationship to the involved multidisciplinary team members. The teams are working together with their own assortment of puzzle pieces, and our goal is to recognize that we are using separate images as guides to interconnect our respective fragments, which results in a distorted mosaic.

In practical terms, we need to assemble a 3D Prioritization team with all the player positions whose combined efforts produce the system results; we need all the puzzlers with their pieces. The breadth of player inclusion must align with the scope of the problem we're investigating, which often results in a larger 3D Prioritization team than we might initially envision. For example, suppose we are trying to improve the discharge efficiency of patients from a Hospital Medicine unit. In that case, we must include core care team members such as physicians, advanced practice professionals, nurses, pharmacists, physical therapists, care transitions, and, when possible, patients.

We also must include clinical support and operations staff, such as environmental services, transport, and patient placement. If we were trying to improve on-time airline departures, our corresponding selection would include gate agents, flight crews, passengers, ground support, maintenance, and flight logistics.

Understanding the Structure and Rules of the Game

We named 3D Prioritization for our use of three steps, Discover, Distill, and Define, which empower teams to move collaboratively from uncovering the complex tangle of systems issues to identifying and prioritizing the critical improvement themes. At an introductory level, the 3D Prioritization steps are simple and user-friendly: *Discover* refers to our collecting team issues related to the systems problem; *Distill* is where we compile and organize the collected issues into themes; and *Define* is how we prioritize the themes in order of importance. The familiarity with these descriptions readily pulls in new-methodology skeptics, who will often comment and be reassured that 3D Prioritization is the same brainstorming process they use in their conventional improvement approaches. We don't try to challenge their assertions (no conflict!) and thank them for participating. We let the process speak for itself, understanding that the power of 3D Prioritization resides in how we set up and apply these three steps to get from conflict to the Critical 20%.

Being mindful of our innate predisposition to approach problems in conflict, we have designed 3D Prioritization to incrementally build and strengthen the trusting team relationships required for us to get to our key transformation targets. At the outset of the 3D Prioritization exercise, we introduce a few basic rules of engagement that aim to promote team participation, reinforce our focus on systems issues rather than individual blame, limit our propensity to solution jumping, and ensure that everyone can be heard. These serve as our guardrails for creating a safe learning environment and conditions for problem solving together.

3D Prioritization: Rules of Engagement

 Everyone is invited to contribute

 "Issues" should be brief thoughts (about the length of a tweet)

 It's about systems, not individuals

 Don't jump to solution

 It is okay to repeat issues or reframe what your colleague has said

DISCOVER—CAPTURING ISSUES AND CONCERNS RELATED TO THE SYSTEMS PROBLEM

When we kick off with the Discover step, we need to pose a question that casts a wide enough net for all to openly share their subjective and objective challenges. For example, we might start the Discover step with a Hospital Medicine team by asking, "What are the issues and concerns related to timely discharge on your unit?" For an airline team, the Discover question might be, "What are the issues and concerns related to on-time departures?" Notice how our use of "issues and concerns" invites participants to share their associated stressors or conflicts and how broad the range of responses to the topic can be.

In addition to issues we might expect, like frustration with last-minute communication, lack of service coordination, and staffing shortages, participants might also bring up less visible issues, such as the inconvenience of remote employee parking, catering delays, or inadequate wheelchair availability. We capture and document every contribution, large, small, and redundant, on a visible display for all to see until everyone has been heard, sharing is exhausted, and the team falls silent. As the Discover process progresses, we increasingly appreciate the complexity and reach of the systems problems across our team activities and our narrow interpretations of what we think is going on. Team members who have been working side by side for years often realize how little they know about each other's roles, and we get an inkling of the core challenges we all face. Beneath the dysfunction and stress, we realize that we're doing our best to collectively achieve the same objective. By capturing all the issues and concerns that matter to the team, we see collaborative problem solving as the way out of the mess. We're creating an opening for something new. Depending on the magnitude of the problem, it is not uncommon at the end of the Discover step to have collected one hundred to two hundred issues and concerns that we then need to organize into categories.

DISTILL—ORGANIZING THE ISSUES AND CONCERNS INTO THEMED CATEGORIES

The Distill step follows Discovery, where we help the team group the collected issues and concerns into common categories. Our objective is to empower team members to discover similarities between the issues and concerns without predetermined category names. This is important because we want to promote open inquiry and the opportunity for us to organize the challenges outside of the box beyond our usual constraints.

Beginning with one issue or concern, participants are invited to identify another issue or concern that appears to be aligned. Without being overly explicit in labeling the relationship, the team has to discuss and collectively agree on the match for it to stick. The categorization continues with selecting and approving additional issues or concerns related to the prior selections until all agreed-upon matches have been identified for that category. The team then proceeds with the creation of the next category using the same approach, and the process continues until all of the issues and concerns have been assigned to categories.

While the categorization process is straightforward by description, the power of the step resides in getting us to listen attentively to each other and becoming aware of the innate assumptions that inform our interpretations and decisions. We further appreciate the limitations of our perspectives, and a category match that seems obvious to one member suddenly invites collaborative consideration. Using the example of issues and concerns from above, a nurse might propose that "lack of service coordination" is related to "catering delays" based on their experience that many patients request a meal before they leave the hospital. A participant from food services might alternatively propose that "catering delays" are more aligned with "last-minute communication" because of the lead time they need for meal delivery. Both perspectives are valid, and we must collectively determine which combination seems most fitting. Perhaps they *all* fit together.

Let's say the team recognizes they don't do a great job planning dietary requests, and they match "lack of service coordination" with "catering delays." Notice how, at this point, we could all have different ideas about the category. It could be very specific to catering, it could be more broadly related to support services, or it could be about generally inadequate team planning. If our train of thought is on support services, a patient care assistant might propose that "wheelchair availability" also fits in this category. The team might agree, or someone from transport services might point out that there aren't enough wheelchairs to meet demand, which could create a different category. Again, the team must grapple with these inputs and collectively agree on how they interconnect.

Regardless of the number of issues and concerns collected in the Discover step, we typically end up with a maximum of eight categories. This reflects the team's growing ability to see the common relationships connecting the issues, concerns, and, importantly, each other. The final task in the Distill step is for the team to name the categories into actionable themes. By category, we invite the team to review the grouped issues and concerns and to iteratively refine the name, typically in the form of a short goal-oriented phrase, until everyone agrees on the fit.

Like the categorization process, participants have multiple perspectives on the theme, and we usually have a lively discussion to get to the agreed-upon result. There are typically several subtopics within the categories, and our objective is to capture them all using a common theme name. Building on the example above, let's assume that we have combined "last-minute communication," "lack of service coordination," and "catering delays" into the same category. We must develop an overarching theme, which may emerge as "Optimize timely multidisciplinary discharge planning." Another category might include "staffing shortages" and "remote employee parking," and this theme might become "Enhance staffing recruitment and retention." The themes we create are high-level and broad, but we have collectively refined the convoluted problem into one we can digest and solve. With our list of themes complete, we must define where to focus.

DEFINE—RANKING THE THEMES IN ORDER OF IMPORTANCE

Define is the last step of 3D Prioritization. At this point, we have collectively dissected the numerous fragments confounding the problem, sorted the puzzle pieces into manageable buckets, and clearly named the identified areas needing improvement. Based on the systems principles we've learned, we know that all identified themes are connected and that, based on Pareto's Law, addressing 20 percent of the themes will solve 80 percent of the problems.

Our objective in the Define step is to collectively identify those Critical 20% themes, and we begin the process by challenging the team to choose a single theme to focus on if they could only work on that one. You can imagine the initial feeling of disbelief that ripples through the team as they try to envision how they will be able to align around one theme and how this singular focus will result in meaningful change. If we were using a conventional brainstorming approach that promoted solution development up front, everyone would cling to their separate ideas, and creating team alignment would be near impossible.

In contrast, observe how we apply the Discover and Distill steps to move the team toward increasing awareness and collaborative problem solving as we tighten the task guardrails. In Discover, we learn to listen to each other as we share issues and concerns, recognizing that we're all in this together. In Distill, we're strengthening our abilities to listen and collaboratively organize the issues and concerns into flexible categories, which intensifies as we name the categories as themes. When we get to Define, we are actually well poised to identify the Critical 20% themes, and by pointing out what the team has already accomplished and reminding them that every theme is connected, we reinforce our sense of empowerment to get the Define step done.

We are careful to emphasize that identifying the Critical 20% themes should be based on what the team regards as the most important themes for us to work on rather than what is most important for system functionality; they are not always the same. This can be a nuanced distinction, and we can use the two example themes above to illustrate the point. Let's assume that we have narrowed our top theme selection to "Optimize timely multidisciplinary discharge planning" or "Enhance staffing recruitment and retention." Both themes are important and connected, so which one should we pick? The answer depends on both of these opportunity gaps' impact on the team's ability to achieve the necessary systems results.

If multidisciplinary teams can't be consistently deployed because of staffing shortages, the priority could be around recruitment and retention; if the multidisciplinary teams are relatively stable but stretched, and departments are actively recruiting additional staff, the priority will likely be in optimizing the team discharge planning process. Regardless of the team's top choice, the interrelationship of both themes will require us to address key components that also involve and impact the second theme. For example, our focus on optimizing team discharge planning affects working conditions and staff retention; alternatively, if we prioritize recruiting and retention, consistent staff availability will likely enhance our optimization of team discharge planning. Both approaches enable us to improve departure efficiency and our functional problem. We're looking for team ownership and the biggest bang for our buck.

When we've collectively agreed upon the top theme, we continue prioritizing the remaining themes, paying close attention to the intensity of their interconnections. The Critical 20% are typically comprised of the top two themes, which, as we observed in the previous example, have tight interconnections requiring coordinated action, and we will largely resolve the remaining cascade of themes by solving the Critical 20%. When we have completed the Define step, we invite the team to do a final gut check by answering two questions: First, do the themes we've identified collectively capture the scope of the problem we're investigating? Second, do we see how our focus on the Critical 20% themes will address key components of the remaining themes? Our collective affirmation sets the stage for the next phase of PrecisionPS.

3D Prioritization Steps: Discover, Distill, Define

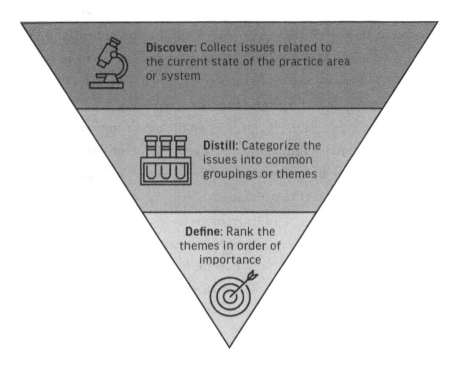

Discover: Collect issues related to the current state of the practice area or system

Distill: Categorize the issues into common groupings or themes

Define: Rank the themes in order of importance

Compassionate Facilitation—Turning 3D Prioritization into a Power Tool

As an avid photographer, I am always bemused when people say, "Your camera takes great pictures." The advances in digital camera technology, ease of use, and accessibility have routinized picture taking and diminished our interest in understanding and applying the fundamental principles of photography for creating consistent, exceptional results. Similarly, one of the transgressions with our use of conventional improvement methodologies, such as Lean and Six Sigma, has been our dissociation of the tools from their core principles.

For example, many quality improvement teams deploy Lean as an isolated improvement toolkit for finite projects rather than applying

Lean as a management paradigm as Deming intended. Training and proficiency revolve primarily around technical tool competencies with the expectation that the tools will deliver great outcomes. Point and shoot—sound familiar? Every once in a while, we get a serendipitous impactful result, and the rest of the time, we produce marginal and transient outputs.

The power of 3D Prioritization is derived from the synergistic coupling of our user-friendly 3D Prioritization tool to the core Precision Problem Solving principles. As facilitators, we serve as the conduit connecting the power source to the tool, catalyzing the team to strengthen and solidify their connection as the 3D Prioritization phase progresses. The takeaway message should be very clear: technical capability alone for using the 3D Prioritization tool is not enough to create conditions for transformative change. Rather, our facilitation is based on our understanding and ability to integrate the Precision Problem Solving principles, which empowers teams to problem solve together to create the new. Let's circle back briefly and look at the key role that our facilitation plays in turning 3D Prioritization into a power tool. We'll be able to appreciate how the principles we've explored in sections function holistically in practice. Everything is connected.

ESTABLISHING A SAFE LEARNING ENVIRONMENT

When we kick off a 3D Prioritization exercise, we are fully aware as facilitators that new teams will show up with a conventional problem-solving mindset that is typically skeptical, change averse, and prone to reactive solution jumping. We are also mindful that change is personal and that the cyclic relationship between fragmentation, conflict, and change strongly influences our behaviors and actions. With this team dynamic as our baseline, our challenge is to apply the Precision Problem Solving principles to create conditions for active engagement.

As described in the 3D Prioritization steps, the level of active engagement is incremental, beginning with our collective sharing of issues and concerns and arriving at a collaborative agreement on the themes that matter most to the team. We compassionately address the stress and frustration that team members experience with systems processes and each other, and we share the systems principles, like the 94% Rule, to redirect commentary toward systems rather than individuals. In the process, we emphasize that everyone's perspective matters and that to understand and solve the problem, we need to hear and capture the issues and concerns of as many people as possible. Our combination of caring about team member well-being, enabling participants to openly share their concerns and expertise without judgment or assumptions, and documenting every contribution for all to see in real time begins to break down misperceptions and foster the essential trusting relationships for safe learning.

Many facilitation pointers can be prescriptively applied, like using verbal regulators such as, "Great point," or, "Thanks for sharing," which acknowledge and validate participant contributions. Facilitation takes practice, and ultimately, the hallmark of masterful facilitation is compassionate authenticity and actually caring about the teams we work with. Facilitation is more about being than doing.

Here's an example of compassionate facilitation related to discharge efficiency during the Discovery step. A team member says, "If leadership cared about us, they would give us on-site parking spots." Sensing the contributor's stress, the personally directed insinuation, and the suggested solution, the facilitator responds, "Thanks for sharing. That sounds like a really frustrating concern. We know we are all doing our best to control what we can, and I'm wondering whether you can share the systems issue behind your suggestion for on-site parking; even when we have a good solution, we want to understand what's going on first." With the redirect, the team member rephrases their comment to, "Remote parking is so inconvenient here, so I'm always late," to which we respond, "Great, let's capture that on the board." The participant has been listened to and the team is reassured that we're focusing on systems problems rather than individuals and collecting issues rather than proposed solutions.

LEARNING TO LOOK

Removing our External Blinders: We learned in the last chapter that the magnitude and corresponding resistance to change is personal. The closer the change gets to us, challenging our personal values, expectations, and behavior, the greater our conflict and the likelihood of digging our heels in and pushing back. If we're going to successfully bring team members together to collaboratively explore and identify sensitive themes, we have to get there gradually with great care.

Our best shot with initial team engagement is to invite sharing about issues and concerns that matter to them and are far enough removed to provide a protective personal cushion. As an integral part of creating a safe learning environment, a key message we convey to teams at the outset of Discovery is for us to blame the systems rather than each other personally for the problems we experience; reflect on how this applies to the remote parking example above. Notice how we applied systems principles and how Discovery is about sharing without a request for responsibility or personal change. As participants describe issues and concerns from differing perspectives, most of us start to recognize the expertise that everyone brings to the table, which slowly lifts the fog limiting our perceptions. With the introduction of integrated Precision Problem Solving principles during Discovery, we enable teams to open the blinders narrowing our perspectives and see a broader view of our systems and teams.

Removing our Internal Blinders: We have intrinsically structured the 3D Prioritization steps for teams to progressively funnel the myriad of complex issues and concerns down to their Critical 20% themes. Our facilitation enables a concurrent movement of self-awareness within team members, which prepares and empowers us to complete the increasing collaborative demands of 3D Prioritization. Again, the process begins at a safe distance, where at the outset of Discovery, we become aware of the limitations of our individual perspectives. We see that what we think *is* and *should be* can also be viewed from other valid angles.

We may not have realized, for example, that our frustration with a teammate's tardiness is due, at least in part, to their remote parking challenge. As team members continue to share issue after concern, we become aware of how we relate to many of them ourselves. We see that we have opinions about everything, which creates stress and conflict.

For example, we want to get patients discharged by 1:00 p.m., but we don't have enough time in the morning to see all our patients before team rounds. We certainly can't reschedule our noon conference for the afternoon. Why do patients need lunch before they leave anyway? Interesting things start to happen as this percolates in our heads. The similarities underlying our frustrations and challenges become evident, and, importantly, we rediscover the core passion and objective that brought us to our profession to begin with: we care about who we serve and what we do. We become aware that we can find a way to take great care of our patients and our wellness if we put our differences aside and align around the functional problem, which is sitting there like a diamond in the rough. It's quite inspiring for us as a team to have that "aha" awakening to a common purpose and interconnection that has been dormant and to collectively rekindle our commitment to problem solving together: open inquiry with no hypothesis.

The Critical 20%—Our Potent Synergistic Output

Getting to the Critical 20% themes is the convergence point of 3D Prioritization, and it's worth ensuring that we understand the multi-level value that the Critical 20% provides and, importantly, how our facilitation of 3D Prioritization gets us there. Remember the *approach* to problem solving is more important than the problem itself.

Understanding Systems: At its most visible and practical level, our identification of the Critical 20% reflects systems opportunities that matter most to the team; we've prioritized our issues and concerns into defined areas needing the highest level of attention and understanding. We understand how the Critical 20% interconnects with other systems components and appreciate our focus on dedicating our valuable time and effort to areas and activity generating the highest return on our investment.

In contrast to conventional problem-solving approaches that prioritize *solution* development up front, our use of 3D Prioritization defines the Critical 20% as problem areas needing further *understanding*, which ensures that our ensuing solutions will be on target. For example, conventional brainstorming might capture the issue of "wheelchair availability" as, "We need more wheelchairs." In contrast, a 3D Prioritization output to the same issue would be more like, "Optimize patient transport capability," which guides us in understanding how wheelchair availability affects efficiency; it could be related to inventory, preventive maintenance, staffing shortages, or something else—we need to look before we leap to a solution. We apply 3D Prioritization to define the Critical 20% anytime we are unclear about what matters most.

TEAM COLLABORATION—PROBLEM SOLVING TOGETHER

Team building is less visible, and we've seen how our facilitation of 3D Prioritization exposes the complex morass of our fragmentation, conflict, and obscured functional problems. To see the functional problems, we must become aware of how our perceptions generate conflict and how this distracts our individual and collective attention. Getting to the Critical 20% is the output of our shared effort in creating a safe learning environment and developing increasing awareness of our integrated relationship with organizational systems, our teams, and ourselves. The Critical 20% reflects our restored capability for collaborative inquiry, our readiness to let go of rigid perceptions, and a solidifying foundation for problem solving together as we progress with Precision Problem Solving.

WHAT MAKES THE CRITICAL 20% THE CRITICAL 20%?

I can recall multiple instances during my prior years of clinical training and consulting where the answer to my asking why something was done in a particular way was, "Because we've always done it this way." It's easy to accept things without inquiry, and it strikes me how our nonchalance creeps in around truisms. Case in point: the Critical 20%.

We know that our prioritized themes are an accurate targeting indicator for our transformation efforts, and we call them the Critical 20% because they align with Pareto's 20/80 Rule. Here's the rub: we're explaining our prioritized themes as critical rule-abiding outputs without understanding how we actually come up with them. While this doesn't detract from our derived value of the Critical 20%, we have seen repeatedly that our core understanding of relationships provides us with clarity and insight to take correct action.

So, let's explore whether we can tap the root of the Critical 20%. Based on our understanding of personal change, could a Critical 20% theme be determined by the collective intensity of our fragmented perceptions and conflict that we experience for an identified theme? Put another way, is a Critical 20% theme one that concurrently impacts us personally and where our ability to understand and solve the problem area is impeded by the myriads of misaligned workarounds we simultaneously deploy? We can't solve the problem individually, which creates enormous cumulative stress and frustration, drawing us together to define it as a critical theme requiring collaborative attention.

For the theme, "Optimize timely multidisciplinary discharge planning," consider how many team members, activities, and schedules need to be coordinated and adjusted to make this work in a busy hospital. We're all working our tails off, stressed and frustrated, and putting our workarounds into action, all with very little return. The problem envelopes us daily, and there's no way we can fix it individually. 3D Prioritization empowers us to collectively identify those critical problem areas where we clash the most and where we must work collaboratively to understand and solve the problem.

Precession as Our Hidden Operative

There is one more phenomenon for us to be aware of within 3D Prioritization that underlies our active engagement on the pressing systems problems we encounter daily. Our facilitation of 3D Prioritization focuses on the tangible issues and concerns that team members experience daily, and we've seen how we use the prioritization exercise to identify the critical themes requiring deeper understanding and action. We've also observed how our facilitation of 3D Prioritization using Precision Problem Solving principles creates conditions for teams to move from collegial interaction to collaborative empowerment, which sets us up for problem solving together.

We've described facilitation as the critical catalyst synergistically coupling the 3D Prioritization tool to the PrecisionPS power source, but we've left out the underlying phenomenon by which the synergy occurs: precession. Our facilitation plays an essential part in *creating conditions* for team collaboration and problem solving together, but it is not the direct source of transformation. We can think of our facilitation as similar to a clinician who is treating a patient for a major medical condition. Whether it's medical or surgical, the clinician will create conditions for healing by initiating a critical treatment intervention with the patient, and it is the patient's physiologic and emotional energy that creates the outcome by precession.

Why does this matter? While precession is typically used with positive connotations, we can see that it actually has no set direction; it sits as much behind great facilitation and great clinical care as it does behind the law of unintended consequences. Remember the Perfectly Designed Rule, where everything is perfectly designed to deliver the result it gets? Precession at its finest.

Here's the nugget: if we understand the nature of precession, we can harmonize with it to create conditions for transformation. If we're unaware, we attribute our actions and outcomes to good or bad luck. It certainly took me a long time to see this; hopefully not for you! Our design and use of 3D Prioritization, coupled with the Precision Problem Solving principles, create conditions for precession to powerfully generate positive transformation. We can't impose transformation on anyone, but we can create opportunities to let go of our perceptions and look at what's actually happening. That's a powerful beginning.

In the next section, we will explore and understand how our identification of the Critical 20% and our nascent ability to problem solve together inform our ability to understand what's actually going on and how to create functional, sustained solutions.

Chapter 10

Understanding Current State and the Functional Problem

You can know the name of a bird in all the languages of the world, but when you're finished, you'll know absolutely nothing whatsoever about the bird. So let's look at the bird and see what it's doing—that's what counts.

—RICHARD FEYNMAN

Let's take a moment to see where we are. We've completed the 3D Prioritization process and have collaboratively identified the Critical 20% themes that we will use to guide us in the second phase of Precision Problem Solving: understanding the current state and what is actually happening in the field. There are a few items for us to be aware of as we proceed:

- As we delve into the actual systems problems, we will expose raw and sensitive breakdowns, much like a clinician removing an old dressing covering a chronic, nonhealing wound; we can trigger a lot of discomfort and resistance in the dressing removal, the wound examination, and the debridement. It's one thing to talk about pain points and another to be hands-on.

- While the Critical 20% themes provide us with a prioritized entry point of inquiry, our theme content is still an unsolved puzzle with a complex assortment of pieces comprised of assumptions, facts, and ideas. Not only do we have to sort through the pieces to identify those that are actually relevant, but we also have to see the big picture to correctly connect them all.

- Our investigation of the current state will continually reveal a myriad of improvement opportunities with multiple inter-connections and feedback loops. If we're not attentive, we will easily become overwhelmed and follow tempting change pathways that divert us off the direct road to understanding the functional problem, like winding scenic routes that take us way off course and add significant travel time.

As daunting as it may seem, the good news is that we have already learned the three core components for tackling these challenges successfully, and we'll continue to use these as an integrated foundation for all our subsequent Precision Problem Solving activities:

- *Our understanding of fragmentation, conflict, and change* provides us with a heightened awareness of our inherent misperceptions, which distort our observation of the functional problem and hinder our ability to solve it collaboratively. Our investigation will expose misperceptions and stir the emotional pot, so we engage with sensitivity and without judgment or assumptions.

- *Our understanding and ability to couple the synergies of the PrecisionPS principles* to tools like 3D Prioritization empower us to break through our individual trepidations and collectively share issues and concerns that interconnect us across organizational, team, and individual levels. We know that we have to see our integrated contribution to chaos and that we have to create a safe learning environment for collaborative problem solving.

- *Our understanding and use of 3D Prioritization* for problem solving together and identifying the Critical 20% serves as our ongoing collaborative prioritization rubric. We always work as integrated interprofessional teams and apply the Discover, Distill, and Define steps to ensure that our problem-solving activities, macro or micro, remain on target. "When in doubt, 3D it out." Let's look at how these integrated components guide and support our investigation of the current state.

Leveraging Conflict:
PrecisionPS Principles and 3D Prioritization

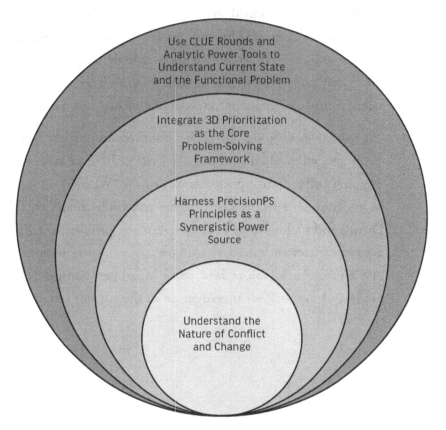

Use CLUE Rounds and Analytic Power Tools to Understand Current State and the Functional Problem

Integrate 3D Prioritization as the Core Problem-Solving Framework

Harness PrecisionPS Principles as a Synergistic Power Source

Understand the Nature of Conflict and Change

Objective Observation: Uncovering Informal Processes

I am the primary cook in our household, and it is very rare for me to find a recipe that guides me to a palate-perfect result. Sometimes, the author leaves out critical steps because they assume we know how to do it, like, "Make a roux," to thicken a sauce. Other times, they call for kitchen appliances or special ingredients we don't have, such as a double boiler or gochujang paste. So, what happens? We do our best with improvisation and workarounds, and while the result might taste good, it's our variation to a leading practice and a dish that will come out different every time. Notice how this creates conflict for the cook and the diners—what we make is never what it should be, nor is it ever the same.

Cookbook recipes are similar to clinical care guidelines and standard operating procedures in that they all define what we should follow to achieve a desired outcome. We use the term "formal processes" to describe how processes are *supposed to* work to get the intended result. As we saw in the example above, there are many instances where, despite best intentions, we don't follow the formal process and instead use modifications, producing inconsistent results. We use the term "informal processes" to describe how our processes *actually* work. As we also saw in my prior clinical training examples, we all simultaneously create our own informal processes to make things work. This further increases variability and inhibits our collective ability to uphold quality, safety, and performance. The inconsistency and fragmentation create confusion and conflict, which crushes our well-being and accelerates our downward spiral.

Why does our distinction between formal and informal processes matter? Interestingly, for all the havoc we create with our workarounds, our informal processes are largely invisible. We tend to look at our dysfunctional environment through the lens of formal processes, blaming the "recipe" for the problem, which frames our workarounds as solutions. Further, when we try to assess where the problem spots are, we continue to use the formal process as our comparative reference; it doesn't occur to us to look at how our interpretations of the recipe contribute to the unintended result. See what naturally happens: our misdirected assessment of the current state is conducted against the ideal, the formal process, which innately leads us to jump to solutions based on *what we think should be* rather than understanding why and what we're actually doing.

For example, let's say the recipe I'm following calls for a double boiler to make a sauce. I don't have one, nor really see the need for it, so I use a regular saucepan instead. I overheat the saucepan, and my sauce sticks to the bottom, which burns it a little and makes it lumpy as I try to stir it back together. Nobody's happy with the result, and we immediately attribute the unintended result to not having a double boiler rather than understanding why I'm using my workaround and what it's supposed to accomplish.

I buy a double boiler, but it's too tedious to use, so I continue to make sauces my usual way; my results get slightly better with repetition, and once in a while, there's a culinary mishap. Everyone assumes I'm using the double boiler, albeit not very well, and before we know it, I've assimilated my informal process into my cooking routine, variation and all. It's no longer visible. When we apply this example of informal process implementation to other formal systems, we see how easily we equate our workarounds with process improvement despite the ongoing dysfunction they create. Our change efforts are more, better, different—incremental solutions destined to perpetuate workarounds, variation, and conflict because we're not attentive to what's actually happening.

Here's the take-home message: we have to expose the informal processes to understand the current state and identify the functional problems, and to do that, we have to break our cycle of "conflict solving" where we continually compare *what we think is* with *what we think should be*, the ideal. That means we must observe what's happening without preconceived ideas, assumptions, or judgment. Informal processes are messy, and as the saying goes, "The devil is in the details." To uncover the informal processes, we must get into the frontline trenches, roll our sleeves, and explore without hypothesis.

CLUE ROUNDING—MAKING THE INVISIBLE VISIBLE

There is no better place to understand what is happening than to be immersed in the frontline action. We routinely shadow teams as part of our conventional improvement methodologies and generally use observation as a standalone point-and-shoot tool rather than a precision instrument applied with care and attention. When we examine our routine observation approach, it is readily evident how limited our visibility range is.

Reflect on how common it is for us to go into a work area as improvement "experts," armed with quantitative data we think defines the problem and using qualitative review to validate our predetermined hypotheses. Consider how we structure our observations in terms of scope, timing, length, and frequency. We set up our observations to look at issues of interest to us, scheduled at our convenience, using flybys that are too brief to see teams in action and without meaningful continuity. In photography, this is analogous to using a zoom lens when we need to capture a broad landscape; the narrow viewing angle and shallow depth of field don't lend themselves to seeing the big picture. We're jumping to a solution, trying to understand a larger systems problem in disjointed snippets. We can also appreciate how teams become frustrated and defensive when we don't take the time to listen to their expertise and attempt to push our preconceived solutions onto their problems. We've seen how this does not create an effective change environment.

Our opportunity to enable transformative change with Precision Problem Solving resides in our comprehensive understanding of what's happening at the front line. In contrast to the conventional assessment approaches we've just described, our PrecisionPS observation process is a collaborative open inquiry with frontline team members, many of whom participated in the 3D Prioritization process. We use their Critical 20% themes as our launch point, which builds a bridge from the 3D classroom to the field with relevant continuity; we begin our observation with frontline team members in areas that matter to them. As mentioned in chapter 6, we've coined the term "CLUE Rounds" for our observation process, which stands for Connect, Listen, Understand, and Engage. Recall from earlier examples how we integrate ourselves into frontline teams as credible colleagues and collaborative learners, observing team activities without assumptions, judgments, or hypotheses. As we explore together, we're building relationships and trust.

Our 3D Prioritization process creates a qualitative heat map with our Critical 20% themes, heightening our awareness and attention during CLUE Rounds. With our Critical 20% themes demarcating hot spots within our observation area, we use CLUE Rounds to develop corresponding relief maps for visualizing the rugged work terrain and the embedded informal processes. Using our photography analogy, CLUE Rounds serve as the wide-angle lens, enabling us to capture our varied systems landscape with breadth and clarity. CLUE Rounds help us accentuate critical systems features that we then zoom in on for a more detailed quantitative look. By going from the big picture to the small, we collectively observe the dysfunction of the broad system and expose our disjointed informal processes that exacerbate our confusion. Because we're collaboratively taking time to observe from big to small without a hypothesis, we're aligned and on target.

CLUE ROUNDING IN ACTION

Here's an example of CLUE Rounds with an inpatient Hospital Medicine care team, where their top Critical 20% theme is "Optimize multidisciplinary discharge planning." We join the team at 7:00 a.m. as the interprofessional members prepare for bedside rounds by separately reviewing overnight events on their established patients and familiarizing themselves with new admissions. Team members arrive on the inpatient unit at different start times, and we begin bedside rounding around 8:00 a.m. when everyone is present.

While we are familiar with the issues and concerns associated with the team's Critical 20%, our goal is to objectively observe how the team progresses through their full rounding routine. As team members get comfortable with our impartial engagement approach, they relax and candidly begin sharing their care challenges. We observe how their intended process of patient rounding, which includes reviewing medications, checking lab results, performing physical examinations, and developing care progression plans, is peppered with frustrating delays and laborious workarounds.

We're rounding with the team on their twenty patients, and they've separately preidentified four patients for possible discharge today. The unanticipated curveballs start flying. One patient was supposed to have a procedure completed the day before, which was canceled because of a last-minute scheduling conflict. They've been placed on the standby list for today, and the team can't advance their discharge planning until the procedure is completed.

The next patient is ready for discharge, and the team is now waiting for a specialty consult service to document their discharge recommendations in the patient's chart; with a resigned headshake, the hospitalist pages the consult service for an update and, after a forty-five-minute callback delay, is told by the consult resident that their attending will see the patient in the afternoon when their morning outpatient clinic has ended.

The third patient is ready to go home and doesn't have a ride because, according to them, nobody told them they were being discharged today; the team social worker sighs and makes a note to explore alternative transportation options for the patient when bedside rounds are complete. And just when we think no patients will be discharged as anticipated, we round on the fourth patient, whose care has progressed smoothly, who feels much better and can't wait to go home; the team has everything set for discharge, and the physician enters the discharge order at 10:50 a.m. as they leave the grateful patient's room. At least we got one out of four out!

It takes us about four hours to round on all the patients, and we finish just before 12:00 p.m., which is perfect timing for the hospitalist physician, who has to peel off to lead an hour-long case discussion with medical residents at their daily noon teaching conference. The care team will spend the afternoon separately following up on their patient care tasks, doing their best to advance patient care and get at least two potential patient discharges home. We thank the care team for sharing their expertise and challenges with us and express our interest in taking deeper dives into the problem areas we've observed together. The team appreciates the time we've taken to see what they do and invites us to join them anytime. We'll be back.

For all the extra effort and variation that we've observed in the team's daily rounding process, this is nothing unusual for them. Their informal processes aren't noticeable until we gently point them out, and their associated frustrations are akin to chronic pain, always present with surges and ebbs. This is their normal way of doing things and enduring. We're working in a very complex environment, and by CLUE Rounding without preconceived hypotheses, we can see how the care team's activities interconnect with systems within and beyond their unit to create unintended consequences; we wouldn't see these interconnections through a zoom lens. Our collaborative team progression through 3D Prioritization and CLUE Rounds is a potent awakening to the informal processes the team has normalized, and with our awareness of the treacherous systems landscape, we can hone in on the critical pain points we need to understand objectively.

MAKING SENSE OF CLUE ROUND FINDINGS— DISCOVER, DISTILL, DEFINE

CLUE Rounds provide us with firsthand exposure to what frontline teams are actually doing and experiencing every day. We participate in CLUE Rounds like a 3D Prioritization field trip. We begin CLUE Rounding using the Critical 20% theme from our 3D Prioritization as the Discovery question for our observations. We uncover various informal processes with the team, which we categorize and Distill into named themes. We then prioritize and Define the CLUE Round Critical 20% themes that need deeper understanding.

In our Hospital Medicine CLUE Round example, we converted our 3D Prioritization Critical 20% theme into the exploratory question, "What are the issues and concerns related to optimizing multidisciplinary discharge planning?" Through collaborative open inquiry, we *discovered* twelve informal processes and outputs while moving through the care team's morning routine, which ranged from different team member start times to a daily midday teaching session that pulled the core team physician off the unit during peak activity. We *distilled* the twelve findings into five themes. We *defined* "Uncoordinated Core Team Discharge Planning" as our CLUE Round Critical 20% theme, with "Misaligned Clinical Care Team Responsibilities and Discharge

Goals" as a close second. Notice how this prioritization process tees us up for our next step of targeted meaningful measurement.

Measurement with Meaningful Process Mapping

Process mapping is one of our primary entry points for delving deeper into our understanding of the functional problem, and we are mindful of avoiding the pitfalls with its use. Like observation, process mapping is used in conventional problem-solving methodologies, and it is again common for us to apply it as a point-and-shoot tool; if we map the formal process steps, we assume the tool will identify key process improvement opportunities. We observe with an intent to process map and frame our observations through a process-mapping lens, which inadvertently narrows our attention from open observation to fragmented snapshots. We overlook a great deal of interconnected detail by building a composite of formal process steps rather than a map accentuating the *critical informal processes.* Our composite winds up depicting intended process steps that eclipse what's actually happening.

Let's say we visit our Hospital Medicine unit to conventionally process map the daily care activities of the care team to identify improvement opportunities. We shadow the team and create a formal process map of their care routine, which includes the following steps: core team members arrive on unit beginning at 7:00 a.m., receive sign-out from overnight coverage, review patient information, update patient care plans, identify potential discharges, begin bedside rounds at 8:00 a.m., evaluate patients and update care and discharge plans, complete care plan activities, orders, and notes, and bedside rounds end at noon.

Our process map describes the team's daily routine in standard steps but doesn't highlight any underlying informal processes contributing to the critical problem. We don't get closer to understanding the root cause of the functional problem, and our map's ambiguity invites us to embellish it with anecdotes, which can steer us in the wrong direction with assumption-based jumps to the solution. For example, we might recall instances where nurses can't attend team rounds because they're too busy dispensing medications, so we recommend hiring more nurses so that their workload is reduced, and they can always round with the care team. The formal process step is documented, but what is actually happening is overlooked. As the saying goes, "We think we're on target but missing the point."

Formal Process Map: Core Team Rounds

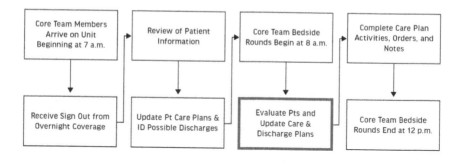

In contrast to conventional process mapping, we use precision process mapping to depict the critical *informal* processes we've defined in our CLUE Round observations, again using the 3D rubric of Discover, Distill, and Define. Our objective is to expose the critical informal processes that we've normalized and highlight their impact on the comprehensive system; we want to make our invisible workarounds undeniably visible. Notice that we are not using process mapping to identify improvement opportunities. Rather, we're utilizing the tool to clarify critical informal processes that we have observed.

In contrast to using conventional process mapping to chart daily team activities and identify improvement opportunities, we use precision process mapping to clarify the informal processes driving our critical CLUE Round theme. This enables us to remain collaboratively aligned and on point. We scrutinize the subset of categorized observations, like puzzle pieces that must be precisely interconnected to reveal the comprehensive picture.

Since we're using our critical CLUE Round theme as our guiding image, we *see* rather than *guess* how the process steps connect; we're clarifying our story rather than looking for a story to tell. Our assembled precision process map deepens our understanding of our informal process by enabling us to see how the interconnected steps functionally impact each other, the larger system, and the output.

Precision Process Map: Uncoordinated Discharge Planning

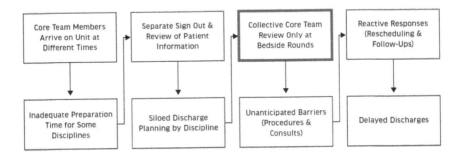

Using our Hospital Medicine CLUE Round critical theme, we review our observations related to "Uncoordinated Core Team Discharge Planning" and see how the informal process of our core team's bedside rounding contributes to unintended discharge delays. Our goal is to describe cause and effect. We map how core team members arrive at their inpatient unit at varied start times, how they get separate patient sign-outs from their respective overnight teams, and how this sets up the core team members to be inconsistently prepared. Each team member shows up to bedside rounds with incomplete information and siloed discharge plans.

As they collectively share their information at the bedside for the first time, it is not uncommon for the core team to get caught off guard with unanticipated discharge barriers, such as procedure cancellations or consult delays, requiring team members to scramble with reactive and time-consuming course corrections. Inevitably, the core team's fragmented and untimely discharge planning contributes to frustrating discharge delays. We apply the 3D rubric to our completed precision process map and define "Fragmented and Mistimed Core Team Rounds" as our next Critical 20% theme.

As we've described, we advance our understanding of the functional problem with precision process mapping by telling a revealing story about the impact of informal processes that the core team can relate to. Reviewing the process map together, we see how seemingly inconsequential steps interconnect to create a cascade of unintended consequences. We're making the invisible steps visible, and on top of that, we're creating awareness about our core team's contribution to discharge delays.

We begin to see that our frustration and assignment of blame for discharge delays to external factors "beyond our control" are partially misplaced. While there is no shortage of opportunities for us to improve the interconnected external systems and processes, such as procedures and consults, we also see that we have ample opportunity to work on unit-based change. We appreciate how our fragmented misperception of *what we think is* and *what we think should be* distracts us from seeing our responsibility for the conflict we create. Sound familiar? Our use of precision process mapping provides us with clarity and direction on where we need to explore further, internally *and* externally, to move beyond conflict and get at *what actually is*, the functional problem. Everything is connected.

Measuring with Meaningful Data and Analytics

Here's a brief recap of our progression in understanding the current state and the functional problem:

1. We start with 3D Prioritization to collaboratively leverage frontline expertise to expose and prioritize their critical issues and concerns relative to our organizational problem.

2. We follow with CLUE Rounds to impartially observe frontline teams in action and uncover the critical informal processes contributing to our problem.

3. We then create precision process maps to clarify the critical informal process steps contributing to our unintended consequences.

Why do we keep going through all of this repetition, you might ask? It's to reemphasize how important it is for us to impartially observe what is actually going on rather than reflexively using tools in a way that limits our field of view from the start. We're creating a critical path of open inquiry in real time from the big picture to the small, and we now have to use meaningful data and analytics to clarify the critical informal process steps and their impact on the functional problem.

Like our preceding steps, we use data and analytics to *clarify* our observations rather than preemptively *identify* problems or validate hypotheses with established data sets, standardized tools, and bench-marks. Data and analytics have high impact when we use them to guide and support the transformation story meaningfully. To achieve this, we apply the same 3D rubric we've used in the prior steps.

We ask the pertinent exploratory question based on the Critical 20% theme from our precision process map and review the inputs defining that critical theme using Discover, Distill, and Define to prioritize our analytic approach. Notice that we are not looking for a needle in the haystack; our prior Precision Problem Solving steps progressively advance our understanding of what matters and where to focus. We also learn a lot about the haystack along the way! Our precision data and analytic approach provide us with focus and the opportunity to innovate. We use organized databases and standard analytics when they provide meaningful information, and when they don't, we explore alternatives and venture into new territory. We don't want to press-mold our story into the shape of predetermined data sets and analytics; we want to use data and analytics to meaningfully guide and support the story as it logically unfolds.

Circling back to our Hospital Medicine scenario, we use our 3D rubric to distill the informal process steps into cause-and-effect categories, which formulates our precision data and analytics question using the preceding Critical 20% theme from our precision process map, "What measures accentuate causes and effects of fragmented and mistimed core team rounds?" We then define "core team scheduling," "discharge criteria," and "procedure and consult completion times" as our critical cause-and-effect analytics. Since we are starting our precision data and analytics with a critical clarifying question rather than established measures, we have to find the right corresponding data sources, which can be challenging. Some of the data we need is automatically recorded and digitally accessible, like inpatient length of stay.

Other data, such as staffing policies and schedules, is available within department-specific databases. Care team guidelines such as discharge criteria may be individualized, highly variable, or undocumented, and data we need for clarifying procedure and consult efficiency may be scattered across multiple databases, including electronic orders, free text progress notes, and financial databases. With our plethora of possibilities, it is easy to appreciate how data access and transparency often emerge as critical barriers to effective improvement initiatives and why we often default to blanket data and analytic approaches when we don't have a precise question to answer. A clinical example of analytic surveillance is our use of total body CT scans to look for clinical abnormalities; our information capture is vast, we're limited to a particular viewing format, and we don't know what we're looking for. When used in isolation, it's not unlikely that we will overlook, misinterpret, or find incidental abnormalities that may or may not be significant. It's not very useful, and we don't have the bandwidth or time to perform this as a routine.

Our takeaway is that meaningful data mining and analytics are intense and tedious processes. We can't customize our analyses broadly, and if we rely on conventional data and analytic approaches to identify problems, the critical areas we're exploring with Precision Problem Solving will not be captured nor on target. We can see why our Precision Problem Solving steps and continued use of the 3D rubric for understanding the current state and the functional problem are critical. When we seek to clarify a problem with precision data and analytics, we take the necessary steps to get down to the right question that informs us where to look—if we're going to put intense effort into extracting data for innovative analytics, we need to be precise.

Advancing the Precision Problem Solving Story: Asking the Right Questions

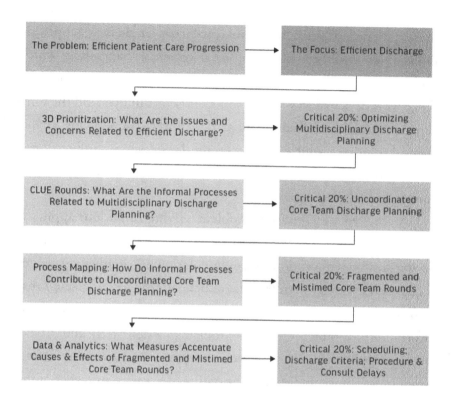

Understanding the Functional Problem Uncovers the Functional Solution

We've put a lot of effort into understanding the nature of conflict and change, the PrecisionPS core principles that empower us to collaboratively problem solve, and how we synergistically connect these foundational components to precision tools that clarify our understanding of the current state and the embedded functional problem. Why do we focus on understanding this when most conventional problem-solving approaches focus predominantly on solution development?

Recall that our fundamental challenge with conventional problem solving resides in our approach to developing solutions based on our incomplete understanding of the problem. We use our fragmented mental models to subjectively interpret *what we think is* happening rather than objectively observing *what actually is* happening, which pushes us to produce solutions based on what we think should be. Since we're attached to what we think and don't understand the functional problem, we reflexively direct our efforts to develop ideal hypothetical solutions, which create piecemeal results and conflict. We're trapped using firefighting and conflict resolution as our problem-solving modalities.

A core tenet of Precision Problem Solving is that our approach to *understanding* a problem is more important than the problem itself. Seeing how our conventional focus on solution development generates the same fragmented results and conflict pattern, we understand that transformation requires a new approach. Rather than focusing our effort on developing solutions to problems we don't fully understand, we investigate the nature of our current problem and *why we haven't solved it*. When we understand the nature of the why and what of the problem, the functional solution innately emerges as the how.

The Approach to Problem Solving Is More Important Than the Problem

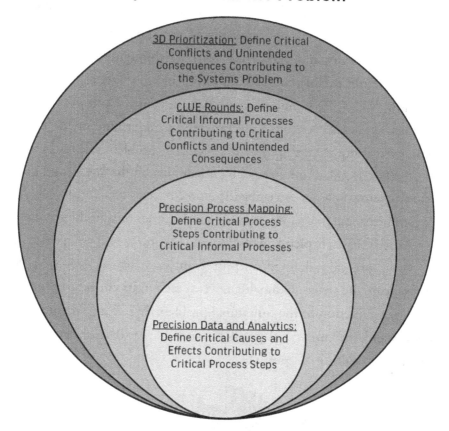

3D Prioritization: Define Critical Conflicts and Unintended Consequences Contributing to the Systems Problem

CLUE Rounds: Define Critical Informal Processes Contributing to Critical Conflicts and Unintended Consequences

Precision Process Mapping: Define Critical Process Steps Contributing to Critical Informal Processes

Precision Data and Analytics: Define Critical Causes and Effects Contributing to Critical Process Steps

We have described in detail how our phased and stepwise progression of Precision Problem Solving informs our investigation from the big picture to the small. We clarify and deepen our understanding of the current state and the functional problem using continually refined quantitative observations and measures. It's easy for us to assume that the functional problem sits at our deepest level of inquiry, and that our ultimate objective with Precision Problem Solving is like any other problem-solving method: to get to the core data set containing the solution. This, however, is not the case!

We do indeed dive deeply into data and analytics to understand the root cause and recall that we do this to *clarify* rather than *identify* the functional problem. The secret sauce to Precision Problem Solving is our comprehensive understanding of the problem that emerges with open inquiry and continuous learning throughout our exploration. We're not peeling back the proverbial onion to get to the source of truth. We're impartially observing and learning about every layer without hypotheses, enabling our progressive understanding to define our inward inquiry precisely. The functional problem resides in the comprehensive picture we create by integrating all the layers, and like a stereogram containing an embedded three-dimensional form within a two-dimensional image, we can only see the functional problem when we absorb the whole picture while looking beyond the superficial detail.

Our precisely defined outputs from each of the PrecisionPS steps create the stereogram, which, when seen in its entirety, reveals a clear 3D depiction of the functional problem. We clearly define and understand the functional problem, and that insight uncovers the functional solution.

Pulling It All Together

Let's see how this plays out when we tell the story of our Hospital Medicine team's problem with efficient discharge.

1. We started by engaging our interprofessional team in a 3D Prioritization exercise. Collectively, we identified a host of issues and concerns related to efficient discharge, which we collaboratively prioritized into themes.

2. We defined "Optimizing Multidisciplinary Discharge Planning" as our critical theme to investigate further, noting a significant amount of team frustration and conflict associated with their fragmented discharge planning efforts.

3. We joined the core team on their inpatient unit to objectively observe what was actually happening as they cared for their patients. Our CLUE Rounds revealed informal processes contributing to inconsistent discharge planning and discharge delays.

4. We observed how core team activities first interconnect during bedside rounds, leading to unintended discharge planning consequences. Collaboratively, we prioritized "Uncoordinated Core Team Discharge Planning" as our critical informal process theme to explore in further detail.

5. We created a precision process map depicting the core team's bedside rounding routine, which includes pre-rounding steps such as differing team member arrival times and reactive responses like inopportune consult follow-ups. Our mapped visualization of their process steps enabled us to collaboratively categorize their critical informal discharge planning

process as "fragmented and mistimed core team rounds," which prompted us to identify measures accentuating the causes and effects associated with critical rounding steps.

6. We selected core team "scheduling, discharge criteria, and procedure and consult delays" as our critical data and analytic measures and quantified these steps' impact on team rounds, discharge planning, and efficient discharge.

Our story goes from big to small and back to big. Everything is logically interconnected, and we have created a Precision Problem Solving stereogram containing the functional problem. When we immerse ourselves in our comprehensive understanding of the discharge efficiency problem, looking beyond the particular details, the functional problem unfolds. We see that uncoordinated discharge planning is linked to the core team's inability to collaborate as a cohesive group to share timely and aligned patient information.

Critical barriers include misaligned core team member schedules, unclear discharge criteria, inconsistent access to patient information, and an absence of dedicated time for collaborative discharge planning. The functional solution becomes evident based on our comprehensive understanding of the functional problem. We must create a core team venue enabling proactive, coordinated, and efficient discharge planning. To be successful, we have to address the identified barriers. The functional solution and its components look obvious and almost seem too simple. However, when we consider the time and effort we invested in understanding the current state, we appreciate the commitment and ownership of the team to this exploration on top of their regular responsibilities.

Reflect on how far we've come. We've created a collaborative problem-solving team that has been engaged and empowered from the beginning. We have defined the critical steps that clarify the current state from big to small, and we all comprehensively understand and can share the story of the functional problem and its solution in a logical, evidence-based manner. Our approach to understanding the problem is more important than the problem itself, and by putting our attention to observing and understanding the why and the what of the actual current state, the functional problem and the how to the functional solution emerge. We are now well positioned to develop and execute a precise implementation plan.

Compassionate Facilitation Has Enormous Impact on Sustainability and Success

With the tangible outputs we've achieved in defining the functional problem and solution using Precision Problem Solving, we need to be aware that our success in advancing our comprehensive understanding is intimately connected to the relationships we build to enable collaborative problem solving. Our ability to create a safe learning environment where we can all show up as learners and objectively explore functional problems without assumptions, hypotheses, and judgment requires us to understand the nature of conflict.

As facilitators, it is essential to know that every team member involved in and impacted by a change initiative is innately in a conflict-solving mindset when we begin. Everyone shows up with their bows and quivers of conflict arrows, ready to let them fly if threats arise. Facilitators are always visible targets, and our understanding of the nature of conflict and our ability to leverage the PrecisionPS principles enable us to remain compassionate, even if and when arrows come our way. We expect them, perhaps feel the sting as they pass through, and yet appreciate that we are not the conflict source. If we get sucked into our conflict and facilitate from there, however, it's game over.

It's worth pointing out one more time how we structure and facilitate our Precision Problem Solving steps to leverage and mitigate conflict. Our use of 3D Prioritization provides a significant redirect from conflict solving in two major ways. Our Discovery question invites team members to share their systems-based issues and concerns and what we think is happening, which empowers everyone to express their subjective sources of frustration and stress. We also refrain from any solution sharing, which is what we think should be happening, effectively shutting down our ability to engage with one another in conflict.

We begin to create a dynamic of introspection into the current state. Even though we are still in the subjective realm of the problem, we're now collectively looking at and listening to how we're thinking about the problem, becoming aware of our deeper similarities. We are creating a safe learning environment for collaborative problem solving and preparing ourselves to advance our inquiry into understanding the current state with objective observation to see what *actually is happening*. Given the power that our use of 3D Prioritization has in keeping us attentive to the current state, mitigating conflict, and defining critical areas of inquiry, we can see why we use the 3D rubric every step of the Precision Problem Solving way.

Changing Direction from Conflict to Collaborative Problem Solving

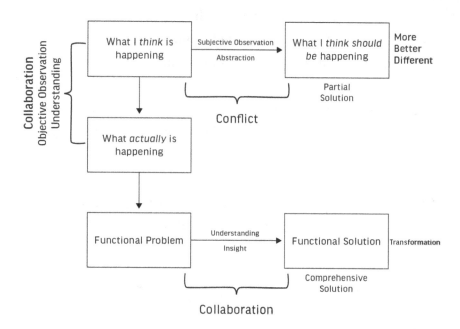

We've learned a lot about the nature of conflict and change and how the intensity of the conflict we experience is proportional to the magnitude of personal change. We've seen how the phases and steps of Precision Problem Solving progressively pull us into awareness about our contributions to the problems we experience and that we will need to change the way we do things. We begin with a relatively detached exploration of systems at the organizational level with 3D Prioritization and advance our inquiry into increasingly personal domains during CLUE Rounds with frontline teams, detailed precision process mapping with team subunits, and data and analytics providing quantified measures.

While our problem solving is never personal, we facilitate teams with mindful awareness of the escalating personal impact that we experience as we move forward. We usually have a conflict intensity threshold that many team members are already close to when we start, and we have to remain beneath that threshold to be collaboratively successful. We facilitate a safe learning environment from the beginning and reinforce our collaborative structure with our activities and compassionate support. Our attention to the current state disrupts the conflict pathway, and our attention to frontline team empowerment, relationship, and understanding creates a strong and sustained foundation for collaborative problem solving.

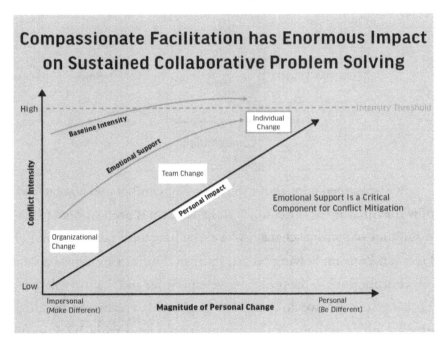

Returning to our Hospital Medicine example, we can appreciate how we become progressively empowered and cohesive as a collaborative problem-solving team in our 3D Prioritization. When we join the core team in their unit with CLUE Rounds, we reinforce our compassionate interest in their work routine through active engagement, objective observation, and awareness. With our precision process mapping exercise, we're dissecting a specific work routine and set this up as a collaborative exercise to clarify how team member activities interconnect to deliver the results they get; we're curious and impartial learners who care. We build on that approach for our precision data and analytics, appreciating that at this stage, our relationships must be trusting, transparent, and committed. We have each other's backs. Our collaborative identification of critical analytic measures helps us to clarify what we've heard, seen, and mapped in prior steps. When we incorporate this information into our composite stereogram, we collectively see the functional problem and its solution and tell our story.

We've collaboratively arrived at our comprehensive understanding of the current state and the functional problem, and we have a clearly defined direction for our functional solution. We are now ready to move to the third and final phase of Precision Problem Solving, in which we will develop, launch, and iteratively improve our functional solution.

Chapter 11

Getting to Action: Iterative Implementation of the Functional Plan

---

There is not first understanding and then action. When you understand, that very understanding is action.

—J. KRISHNAMURTI

In the last chapter, we learned how the Precision Problem Solving steps we take enable us to achieve a comprehensive understanding of the current state and how our synthesis innately reveals the functional problem. Our understanding of the functional problems is objective, factual, and conflict-free. Unlike making a subjective interpretation of occurrences or experiences that we don't completely understand, which drops us into conflict and ideas (*what I think is* and *what I think should be*), the functional problem creates immediate action as the functional solution.

Put a different way, if we don't understand what's happening, we must hypothesize, which puts us in a position to make imprecise choices. If we comprehensively understand what's actually happening, we act. For example, suppose we have a new sick patient with a fever and upper respiratory symptoms who needs treatment. In that case, we must consider multiple factors such as medical history and diagnostic tests, whether to start them on empiric antibiotics or give them Tylenol and a decongestant. In contrast, if an established sick patient comes to us with a fever and is diagnosed with strep pneumonia, we will start them on a specific antibiotic like amoxicillin. Similarly, if we're walking our dog down the street and a car comes barreling toward us, we don't think about what to do. We jump out of the way. When we understand the functional problem, we act.

All of this is to point out that our comprehensive understanding of the functional problem creates immediate insight to the functional solution. As I described in my adverse event with Linda, insight does not happen with effort. It happens by letting go. If you've ever done yoga, it is similar to maximizing a stretch by relaxing rather than forcing our bodies into position. We can't see the 3D form in a stereogram unless we look beyond the composite mosaic and see the composite without all the pieces. This is counterintuitive to our innate tendency to look at the fragmented data we have put together and conjure up ideal solutions, like imagining animal shapes in clouds. The functional solution shows up when we see the functional problem and create the space for insight.

It is not uncommon for us to ask how insight into the functional solution qualifies as immediate action since nothing seems to have tangibly changed. It's difficult to describe, and we have at least two potential explanations to consider. First, as we saw above, insight is not a thought process that takes time with idea generation and choice to arrive at the functional solution; it is immediate, objective, and clear.

Second, the functional solution defines a critical purpose, direction, and outcome. We understand where we're going and what needs to be done, and what remains is for us to build and implement the functional elements and their interconnections to activate the functional system. Relevant personal examples of insight-informed action are when we make sudden and profound lifestyle changes. We might know a longtime heavy smoker who abruptly quit overnight, never picking up a cigarette again; when we ask why, they say that they just woke up one day and realized that it was time to stop, and that was that.

They still need to rebuild their nonsmoking lifestyle, like getting rid of their cigarettes and smoking paraphernalia, managing nicotine withdrawal, and addressing other health-related issues. Still, there is no temptation or thought of going back. The definitive act began with the insight. If we observe, we see similar insight phenomena in small subsets who struggle in areas such as diet, alcohol, and abusive relationships. In contrast to our pervasive attempts to solve our complex problems in conflict, we become aware and move beyond our conflict, see what's actually going on, understand the functional problem, and have an instantaneous insight into the functional solution. We're ready to translate our act of inner transformation into tangible external outputs.

Translating the Functional Solution to the Functional Plan

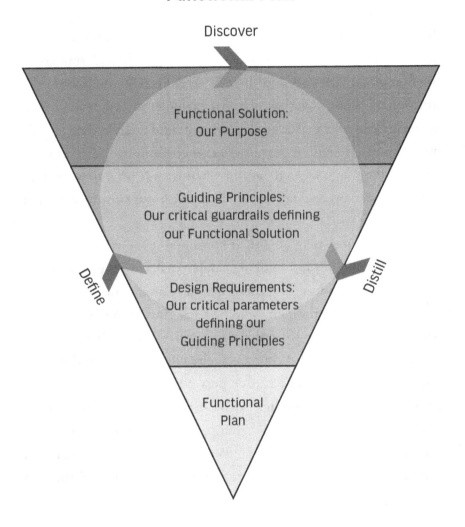

Our Functional Plan Framework— Clarifying Purpose, Guiding Principles, and Design Requirements

Our functional solution needs to be translated into a functional plan for sustained implementation, and it is very helpful to establish a design framework that our teams can reference to ensure that we remain aligned. Remember that while our teams are aligned, we are integrating a functional solution that will have broader organizational impact where we will encounter conflict and functional barriers. Our design framework is important in guiding us with precision implementation, as it enables us to communicate the why, what, and how for the change that will impact our stakeholders.

DEFINING OUR PURPOSE (THE WHY)

We've learned that defining a clear purpose is one of the critical components of a system, and our description of our functional solution is essentially that. Defining the purpose statement is a collaborative team effort, and we continue to apply our 3D rubric, beginning with an appropriate question regarding elements that need to be captured, distilling them into themes, and defining the critical phrase content. The purpose statement has to be meaningful and relevant at the individual, team, and organizational levels.

As we've seen in prior examples, cursory attention can easily diminish its value. Purpose statements can define objectives in powerful ways, particularly when they tap into our subjective sphere of influence. The automotive industry is a good example: BMW's mission is "to move people with products that evoke emotions." On the other hand, Ford's mission is "to help build a better world, where every person is free to move and pursue their dreams." Both companies are addressing the functional solution of moving people, and the rest of the statement defines the subjective attributes they think will appeal to their respective customers and organizations. We can see that these purpose statements will deliver distinct systems outputs for each company and that our clarification of purpose matters.

Let's pull our Hospital Medicine example forward. In chapter 10, the functional solution emerged as "creating a venue for proactive, coordinated, and efficient discharge planning." We bring our team together to discover the important attributes of our functional solution and come up with elements such as being timely, collaborative, proactive, aligned, and action-oriented. We distill and define these elements into critical themes and craft them into our purpose statement, "Collaborative and Coordinated Care Progression from Admission to Discharge." Our clarified purpose resonates powerfully with our team because it's ours, we own it, and it also clearly conveys the why to our functional solution. Our next step is to clarify the guiding principles for our solution design.

Defining Our Purpose

What Should We Emphasize as Important Objectives for Our Function Solution?

DEFINING OUR GUIDING PRINCIPLES (THE WHAT)

Guiding principles are the guardrails that we establish to ensure that our functional solution and purpose are upheld in the design of our functional plan. The objective is to define critical principles that provide high-level direction for our design and output without constraining opportunities for creativity and innovation. We want to ensure that our adherence to the guiding principles of our design will deliver our sustained functional solution. If we take BMW's mission statement, we might create guiding principles such as, "vehicles engineered for exceptional stability and handling in all driving conditions," and, "vehicle designs combining our high standard of quality workmanship with advanced technology." Our guiding principles clarify what "evoking emotions" looks like in a way that still enables designers and engineers to explore and innovate.

Using our Hospital Medicine scenario, our team references our purpose statement and our understanding of the critical themes we captured in our story of the functional problem. We apply our 3D rubric to Discover, Distill, and Define two critical guiding principles: "Care progression aligned with hospital capacity and throughput priorities" and "Collaborative core team engagement in daily transitions of care planning." Like our BMW example, we are clarifying the inclusion criteria for our design, the what, while empowering our team to customize how the specific functional plan elements are created and integrated. Now that we have a defined purpose and guiding principles that our team has developed and owns, we advance to clarifying our guiding principles with more specific design requirements.

DEFINING OUR DESIGN REQUIREMENTS (THE HOW)

We develop critical design requirements as parameters that define our preceding guiding principles. There may be more than one design requirement for each guiding principle, and our objective is to apply them as the pragmatic touchpoints to the functional plan. Design requirements provide the instructional guidelines for the system elements and processes we establish and integrate to provide sustained functional outputs. While our goal is to have a consistent approach for implementation, there is still some flexibility in the design requirements that enables us to make iterative adjustments over time as service conditions evolve and, as importantly, so that we can scale and spread our functional solution and plan to other service areas. We understand that we must customize the functional plan to accommodate inherent distinctions across other service offerings.

Our team again uses our 3D rubric, guiding principles, and comprehensive understanding of the functional problem for our Hospital Medicine unit to define our design requirements. These include, "Align core team staffing and scheduling with optimal core team function," and, "Designate time for the core team to review critical transition of care milestones and barriers." Notice how our first design requirement states that the core team members should coordinate their collective presence to efficiently advance patient care and discharges but doesn't define specific start times or intervals; those are for the service teams to decide.

Similarly, our second design requirement highlights the importance of having dedicated time to review key care progression and discharge readiness indicators while leaving the specifics up to service teams. For instance, unit patients are being treated for a variety of clinical conditions, and a patient with heart failure may be fluid-overloaded and have a discharge milestone of getting back to their baseline weight; another patient may have bad pneumonia and have a discharge milestone of completing a defined course of intravenous antibiotics. Our design requirement is essentially asking our core teams to establish a time to review care progression and discharge plans and to be specific about the treatment targets and the barriers so that every core team member is working together with the same objectives. When this design requirement is combined with our first one, our proviso is to create service conditions for delivering efficient and effective care. We now have what we need to create our functional plan.

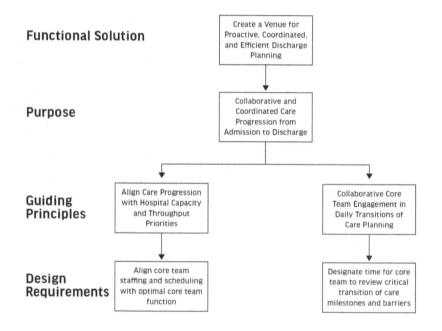

Building the Functional Plan—Our Blueprint for Sustained Transformation

Our attention to clarifying the functional solution using our 3D rubric to define purpose, guiding principles, and design requirements enables us to create a precise functional plan. Our functional plan is our implementation blueprint, our instruction guide specifying the system elements and interconnections we need to build to deliver our sustained functional results. We understand that our functional result is transformational, not the usual more-better-different, and that we are making significant changes.

For all of the success we've created with our collaborative problem-solving capability, we always hesitate to relinquish the status quo, what we know, and how we do things. This is why defining purpose, guiding principles, and design requirements is extremely helpful. We understand where we're headed and stay precisely on track. We often engage our team in focused "flash" 3D Prioritization exercises for select design requirements that involve significant change and offer various functional options. We must take the time and effort to Discover, Distill, and Define our team's inputs into targeted action.

For example, our Hospital Medicine team has to develop a solution to align staffing and scheduling to optimize core team function. Team members start at different times for multiple reasons, and we must understand the why and what for these variations. We know a lot of this from our clarification of the functional problem, and we're now reviewing this with the intent to act.

Our directional alignment from the functional solution to our design requirements empowers us to establish that core team members will be on the unit by 7:00 a.m. This gives our core team adequate time to get sign-out from overnight coverage, review and update patient charts, and collectively meet at 7:30 a.m. for a collaborative transition-of-care huddle to identify potential discharges before 8:00 a.m. bedside rounds.

Using the 3D rubric similarly, our team changes their bedside rounding order to prioritize potential patient discharges and initiate their discharge process by 9:30 a.m. This enables those patients to be discharged by 11:30 a.m. Our team's adjustments and added attention to collaboratively managing shared care progression milestones and barriers enable bedside rounds to be completed by 10:30 a.m., which provides the core team with an additional hour and a half to complete their other care activities. Our team establishes an afternoon huddle at 3:00 p.m. to review their day's activities and update patient care plans in preparation for the night coverage and the next day. Our functional plan is precise and on solid footing, and we now have to put it into action to enable us to make necessary adjustments to achieve sustained, meaningful results.

Functional Plan
Precision Process Map: Collaborative and Coordinated Discharge Planning

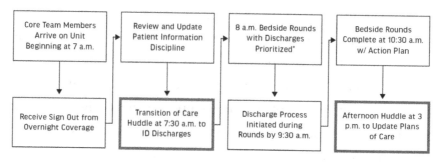

*unstable patients also prioritized

CONTINUOUS FUNCTIONAL IMPLEMENTATION: ACHIEVING SUSTAINABILITY, SCALE, AND SPREAD WITH PDSA

The PDSA cycle is an established tool for continuous improvement that became popular with its introduction by Walter Shewhart and W. Edwards Deming. Unfortunately, we often overlook their rationale for using PDSA, and as we have seen with other tools in our earlier examples, we commonly misuse PDSA as another point-and-shoot tool for identifying and testing solutions to problems that are incompletely understood. We think that churning our ideas through PDSA long enough will somehow enable the tool to produce a desired output. But we can't churn butter without the correct ingredients, and as the saying goes, "Garbage in, garbage out." When we don't get the results we *think should happen,* we dismiss the value of PDSA and resort back to our conventional approach of firefighting and workarounds.

We use PDSA as an integral tool for Precision Problem Solving to clarify and refine our functional implementation iteratively. When we get to the stage of iterative implementation, we already have a comprehensive functional plan for a functional problem defined by *what actually is happening.* Our entry into the PDSA cycle begins with a precise functional plan defined by our Critical 20% priorities at every preceding PrecisionPS step; we're using PDSA, which by its design inherently incorporates the 3D rubric, to iteratively implement a functional plan that is already on target. Using PDSA enables us to activate and measure critical process elements, understand what's happening, and iron out the kinks with corrective action. In contrast to our misinformed use of PDSA to identify, test, and refine ideas, which can result in multiple cycles to generate a useful output, our precise application of PDSA with PrecisionPS typically creates value in two to three cycles.

Continuing with our Hospital Medicine example, our team launches the implementation using a new precision process map, which serves as our initial plan in the iterative PDSA cycle. We engage in CLUE Rounds for several days to observe how our core team members are adjusting to the coordinated start times and how the 7:30 a.m. transition-of-care huddle is working. We discover that the core team is having challenges with efficiently organizing the huddle and that they are running late for bedside rounds by about fifteen minutes, which throws off the subsequent bedside rounding targets.

We use the 3D rubric to examine the transition-of-care huddle issues and discover that roles and responsibilities for discharge planning lack clarity, particularly around patient clinical care and postacute discharge needs. We collaboratively define "medical readiness for discharge" as a critical discharge planning indicator and assign the Hospital Medicine physician to share the indicator for each patient with the team. Our team can now prioritize care activities based on whether patients are medically ready for discharge. When we incorporate this revised functional plan into our next PDSA cycle, we not only improve the time and value of the morning transition-of-care huddle, but we also realize that using the medically ready-for-discharge indicator during the afternoon huddle makes it possible for us to discharge additional patients in the afternoon as well as proactively prepare patients for earlier next-morning discharges. Our use of PDSA has made our precise functional plan even better.

Iterative Implementation:
PDSA Is a Power Tool with a Functional Plan

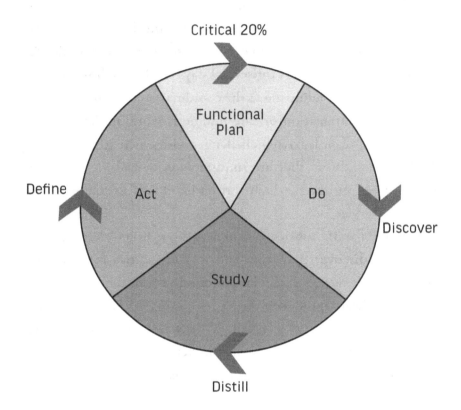

Fidelity of Implementation—Managing Variation and Avoiding Workarounds

As we learned in the previous cooking example, it is very easy for us to skip steps or create workarounds to a recipe, which results in variable outcomes. Our functional plan implementation is subject to the same challenge of variation management. When we don't have meaningful process measures to clarify the vulnerable steps, we are hard-pressed to make functional corrections. Meaningful measures empower us to act rather than admire our problem, and our continued use of CLUE Rounds as part of the PDSA "Study" phase enables us to uncover any informal processes that emerge during implementation.

In contrast to our CLUE Round observations during our current state assessment, where we expect to uncover divergent informal processes from the formal, our functional plan is designed for the informal and formal processes to be the same. What's actually happening is what we plan. Our new current state is dynamic, and as we saw in the corrective response our Hospital Medicine took to improve their transition of care rounds, consistent and attentive use of the 3D rubric in PDSA enables us to observe, measure, and correct informal process deviations with efficacy before they become invisibly permanent.

We can appreciate the critical importance of upholding a consistent and disciplined approach to our iterative implementation process as much as we maintain consistency in our use of the systems and processes we are implementing. Not only is this critical in launching a functional plan in a specific location like a unit, but fidelity of implementation is also crucial when we scale and spread our functional plan to other areas as a leading practice. Even when we customize functional plan elements to align with distinct needs in other areas, we consistently use our Precision Problem Solving principles, our 3D rubric, and PDSA to guide our implementation. We are always on target, and our results are quantified and sustained.

Mastery of Facilitation: Successfully Piloting in the Turbulence of Conflict and Change

Aviation analogies are common in healthcare, and we can apply a flight analogy to our facilitation of Precision Problem Solving as well. Pilot proficiency requires expertise and experience in three major areas, all of which involve constant attention and continuous learning. We must have the technical knowledge and skills to fly the airplane safely during routine flight and in atypical and emergent situations. As automated and technologically advanced as modern aircraft are, pilots must also be able to navigate to their intended destinations, which involves various skills, procedures, and equipment. And third, we need to understand, anticipate, and respond to inclement weather, particularly turbulence. We can't understate the importance of understanding and responding to weather conditions; we can be the masters of technically flying the airplane and navigation, but if we are untrained and inattentive to weather and turbulence, we may not reach our destination, and our outcomes can be disastrous for everyone on board as well as people on the ground.

As facilitators of complex problem solving and transformation, our proficiency requirements have striking parallels. We must have expertise and experience in technically operating our improvement methodologies across multiple scenarios. Facilitators chart and navigate to their intended destinations using established and situationally modified plans. And finally, we have to pay close attention to environmental turbulence manifesting as conflict and change.

For the similar competencies we've highlighted between aviators and facilitators, here's the striking juxtaposition: pilots are required to actively train in understanding and developing competencies in all three areas, whereas the vast majority of improvement facilitators are not. Above all other training gaps, we are profoundly deficient in understanding and managing conflict and change. We may have expertise in the technical operation of our improvement methodology toolkits and knowledge to set a course for an improvement outcome that we think matters. Still, when we don't have situational awareness and the ability to manage conflict and change, we are highly susceptible to encountering unexpected severe turbulence, causing harm, and falling well short of our destination. This is why we emphasize understanding the nature of conflict and change in Precision Problem Solving.

As we have learned in our examination and application of PrecisionPS, our technical expertise, navigation skills, and ability to manage environmental conditions are integrated into functional synergy. We understand that our core principles in systems, participatory management, and peer support drive our functional competencies that empower our teams to create transformational change. Like aviation, we incorporate our understanding of conflict and change turbulence into every tool, step, and phase of Precision Problem Solving. We have seen how the risk and intensity of turbulence, though at times unpredictable, intensify as we advance our initiatives; change becomes increasingly personal, and we need to be ready to respond.

By being prepared for conflict from the start, we introduce safety measures in the form of compassionate support and progressively collaborative tools, actions, and direction setting, which strengthen our relationships, understanding, and ownership for successfully implementing our functional plan. Landing the airplane is one of the most intense phases of flight, where preparation, attention, and team integration are critical. Our final approach with Precision Problem Solving is our iterative implementation of our functional plan, and all our understanding, expertise, and skills converge to safely touch down on our destination runway. Our safe and successful arrival is always a cause for team celebration.

Pilot and Facilitator Proficiency: Synergy

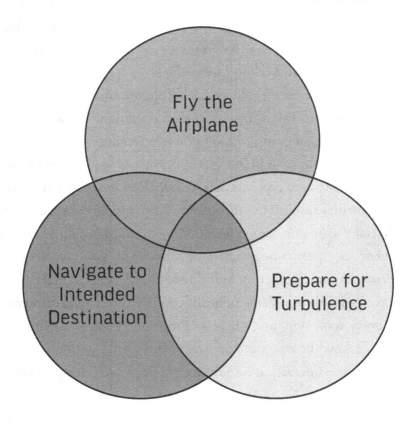

Chapter 12

So What?

A new type of thinking is essential if mankind is to survive and move toward higher levels.

—ALBERT EINSTEIN

We've done an exhaustive exploration in the past eleven chapters to understand the challenges, needs, and opportunities for transformative problem solving. We've shared my self-imposed ordeals and learnings during my personal and professional development as I progressed through our complex and stressed healthcare system. We've painstakingly looked at the relationship between fragmentation, conflict, and change as barriers to observing what is actually happening, understanding our functional problems, and creating sustained functional solutions. We've described how our conventional problem-solving approaches are disconnected from underlying core principles and purpose and how their isolated use as toolkits generates limited results. We've explored our conventional tendency to misunderstand, diminish, and sideline the power of our personal well-being in collaborative problem solving. We've seen how our ideal solutions, based on our retrospective and partial understanding of problems, simply reconfigure prior improvement efforts in the form of more, better, and different.

So, what is the point of all this? Through our shared objective understanding of the current state, we can see that healthcare is in dire need of comprehensive change and that our current approaches, as well-intended as they may be, are not delivering the needed results. As Deming aptly stated, "Management by results is like driving a car by looking in the rearview mirror."[10] We need to move beyond reactive and ideal problem solving to active functional transformation. Learning to Look, Looking to Understand, and Understanding to Act are the fundamental components of transformative problem solving. We have studied the critical existing challenges of conventional problem solving and described the structure of the PrecisionPS methodology using these components. For all the in-depth exploration we've done, we don't want to lose sight of these key points. May our objective inquiry into the following questions clarify our critical takeaways and empower us to create profound compassionate change that renews healthcare and uplifts our lives from surviving to thriving.

---

10   Neil Almond, "Quality. Are You Driving, Using Only the Rear View Mirror?" LinkedIn, November 25, 2021, https://www.linkedin.com/pulse/quality-you-driving-using-only-rear-view-mirror-neil-almond.

1. We're Told That Everything We Do Should Have a Purpose and a Desired Outcome. How Can I Possibly Solve a Problem without a Hypothesis?

We have seen how the approach to understanding a problem is more important than the problem itself, and if we begin by understanding the question, the answer often reveals itself. What do we mean by "purpose" and "desire," and why are these such important drivers in our lives? The dictionary defines purpose as "to put forth; aim; intention," and desire is "to strongly wish for or want."

Pursuing purpose and desire always puts us in a state of wishful becoming, moving from what we think is to what we think should be. Everything we look at is filtered through our interpretations, comparisons, and judgments based on our values, traditions, experiences, and accumulated knowledge. As a result, what we *think is* never reflects *what actually is*, and *what we think should be* is never based on *what actually is* either; our attempted solutions are based on ideas or hypotheses rather than factual understanding. Our fragmented perspectives and partial understanding create conflict, becoming increasingly complex and intense as we try to resolve it. Before we know it, our persistent reactive efforts to "conflict solve" lead us further astray from the functional problem, *what actually is*, and we are lost. We get stressed and trapped in a morass of ineffective workarounds.

THE STORY OF TEN THOUSAND STEPS

Let's say I decide to increase my physical activity because I've heard that walking ten thousand steps daily will reduce my risk of heart disease. My family and friends are doing it; they all have Fitbits and compare themselves to each other. I feel self-conscious about my inactivity, so I decide to join in on the action.

I accessorize and begin my daily ten-thousand-step routine. I enthusiastically stick with it for a couple of weeks, but my work obligations pick up, and I start to fall short of my daily target. I feel bad because I'm failing. "Not to worry," I say to myself, "I'll compensate by increasing my daily steps to twenty thousand when I can." I'm now working toward a weekly ten-thousand-step average. I have a bad hip that starts to bother me more with all the walking, slowing me down, but I refuse to stop—no pain, no gain.

Ultimately, I can't tolerate the pain anymore, and I have to discontinue my walking routine. I see an orthopedic surgeon who tells me I have degenerative arthritis in my hip and that I have to find some other form of activity to avoid surgery. I'm devastated and at a loss for what to do. Then I come across a review article, which points out that the daily ten-thousand-step target we're all captivated by is an arbitrary number and that evidence suggests we can get similar health benefits with far fewer daily steps. I ask myself, "What have I been doing, and how did I get to this?"

If our conventional approach to problem solving is based on conflict and hypothesis, is it possible to change our paradigm and make a transformative course correction? We define conflict as "a subjective contradiction resulting from fragmented comparisons involving status, values, and expectations," and a hypothesis as "a proposed explanation based on limited evidence as a starting point for further investigation." We can see that the common denominator to conflict and hypothesis lies in not seeing *what actually is*, which means our conventional problem-solving approach isn't based on understanding *what actually is* either. Since we mistake *what we think is* for *what actually is* and thereby misunderstand the functional problem, our conventional problem-solving approach is derailed by conflict and dependent on hypothesis, which creates fragmented and suboptimal results. So, if we want to move beyond partial and inconsistent results to a comprehensive solution, we must first see *what actually is.*

To see the functional problem, *what actually is*, we must learn to look without our usual filters. Learning to Look begins with our awareness and understanding of the nature of conflict:

- Awareness that our innate tendencies of interpretation, comparison, and judgment establish our foundation for fragmentation and conflict, limiting our ability to see *what actually is*

- Awareness that our inevitable inclination of jumping to hypothetical solutions based on our limited understanding of *what actually is* exacerbates fragmentation, suboptimal results, and conflict

- Understanding that our ability to look, to clearly see *what actually is*, requires open inquiry, being present as impartial learners without assumptions, conflict, or hypothesis

Learning to Look is the critical foundation for problem solving together. It is about becoming aware of the subjective veil that impairs our vision. Our awareness of the veil empowers us to remove it and objectively see the full spectrum of the common functional problem. When we show up as attentive observers and defer to each other's functional expertise, we are capable of collaborative engagement, comprehensive understanding, and action.

If we now return to the original question, we can see how purpose and desired outcomes can lead us astray when they are subjective rather than objective. Our understanding of the nature of conflict exposes our innate subjectivity, which impedes our ability to see and understand what actually is. When we learn how to look objectively, without constraints or hypotheses, we are open to seeing what's actually going on. Consider how the story of ten thousand steps might have played out differently with this insight.

In seeing all this, perhaps the more appropriate question is, "How can I possibly solve a problem *with* a hypothesis?"

2. How Is PrecisionPS Distinct from Other Improvement Methodologies?

Most conventional healthcare improvement methodologies, such as Lean, have been separated from their fundamental purpose and used in isolation as project-specific toolkits. For example, very few people appreciate that Deming's Total Quality Management (TQM) methodology, from which Lean originated, emphasizes quality improvement as an integrated organizational management paradigm, a cultural way of being rather than doing.

> Our prevailing system of management has destroyed our people. People are born with intrinsic motivation, self-respect, dignity, curiosity to learn, joy in learning. The forces of destruction begin with toddlers—a prize for the best Halloween costume, grades in school, gold stars—and on up through the university. On the job, people, teams, and divisions are ranked, reward for the top, punishment for the bottom. Management by objectives, quotas, incentive pay, business plans, put together separately, division by division, cause further loss, unknown and unknowable.
> —W. Edwards Deming

We've lost the why and the what underlying purposeful improvement and are primarily focused on the how. When we dissociate the core purpose and underlying principles addressing human dynamics and our inherent resistance to change, we mistakenly rely on improvement tools to identify and solve our problems, focusing our training on technical proficiency and operational protocols. This creates a callous and reactive point-and-shoot approach to problem solving. We don't see the comprehensive picture, and our limited and fragmented understanding inevitably requires us to choose solutions based on ideas and hypotheses. Our insular efforts generate suboptimal and unsustainable results.

Let's say hospital leadership is trying to cut costs and has financial data suggesting that significant savings could be achieved in the next fiscal year by reducing the approved budget for nurse vacancies. Their rationale: the nursing department seems to be providing adequate care with their existing limited resources, and it's unlikely that they will be able to fill all the vacancies in the coming fiscal year. So, the hospital leaders cut the nursing vacancy budget by 50 percent. The existing nursing workforce continues to stretch, and the news that vacancies will not be filled exacerbates their frustration and stress to a tipping point, which results in additional staff attrition. The remaining nurses now have to work even harder, quality and patient safety lapses increase, and patient satisfaction scores plummet. The problem is now much worse—penny-wise and pound-foolish.

Like a well-designed machine that requires all its parts to be present, functional, and correctly assembled to operate, Precision Problem Solving is a holistic methodology that integrates the why, what, and how to create transformative outputs. PrecisionPS cannot function as separate components nor without comprehensive facilitator training. While conventional improvement methodologies may incorporate systems and participatory management theory variations into their toolkits, PrecisionPS is distinctively powered by a synergistic triad of systems, participatory management, and peer support principles.

We connect this high-performance engine via compassionate facilitation to the PrecisionPS power tools, which empower our trained teams to create and implement transformative results. Unlike conventional improvement methodologies that develop solutions based on abstraction, we use PrecisionPS to create solutions based on our comprehensive factual understanding of functional problems. As we discussed in the previous question, our biggest challenge in understanding the comprehensive functional problem is our innate inability to see it clearly. This is due to our predisposition to look at everything subjectively in comparative fragments, which limits our visibility and creates conflict; the comparison between what we *think is* and what we *think should be* is our biggest culprit. So, our critical first step in PrecisionPS is "Learning to Look." Before we can see and understand the functional problem, we need to see and understand the nature of conflict.

LEARNING TO LOOK: SEEING AND UNDERSTANDING THE NATURE OF CONFLICT

Conflict is like a poison ivy vine wrapped around the trunk of an oak tree, our functional problem, extending its tendrils along the oak's branches and entangling its leaves within the oak's foliage. We're trying to improve sun exposure to the garden beneath, and we have no idea what the extent of the functional problem is because it's enveloped in conflict, creating a complex and obscure canopy. We naturally blame the poison ivy, what we *think is* causing the problem, and trim back the leaves and stems with conventional pruning tools and techniques, thinking this should improve the sunlight. We're so preoccupied and stressed with our trimming that we don't see our actions' futility as the ivy regenerates and grows despite our laborious efforts.

When approaching the problem with PrecisionPS, our facilitated use of the 3D Prioritization power tool enables us to see the futility of our conflicted actions and mindfully guides us back to the vine, making us aware of the common pathway to and from all the ivy's stems and leaves. We follow the vine down the oak's trunk to the ivy's root, and in seeing and understanding the source, we eliminate the poison ivy completely, exposing the oak tree as it *actually is*. In the absence of conflict, the current state of our functional problem is visible. We are Learning to Look and have created conditions for understanding the current state and the functional problem with impartial observation and problem solving together.

LOOKING TO UNDERSTAND: SEEING AND UNDERSTANDING THE CURRENT STATE AND THE FUNCTIONAL PROBLEM

With our understanding of the nature of conflict and the importance of objectively observing our current state as it *actually is*, we use CLUE Rounds to Connect, Listen, Understand, and Engage frontline teams as they perform their daily activities. Our prioritization of impartial frontline observations before diving into quantitative analytics is a critical distinction. We don't make any prior assumptions or hypotheses that would narrow or distort our scope of inquiry or collaborative problem-solving ability.

We begin by seeing *what actually is* rather than being guided and influenced by its reflection. By directly observing the embedded *informal* processes, seeing *what's actually* happening versus what *should be ideally* happening, we then use process mapping, data, and analytics to *clarify* rather than *identify* the critical elements contributing to

215

the functional problem. Our collaborative understanding of the comprehensive story through all levels of inquiry reveals the functional problem, like a stereogram hiding a three-dimensional object within a two-dimensional mosaic. Our objective understanding of the comprehensive functional problem creates conditions for the precise functional solution.

UNDERSTANDING TO ACT: INSIGHT AND ACTION TO IMPLEMENT THE FUNCTIONAL SOLUTION

In distinction to conventional problem solving, where teams spend considerable time and effort generating abstract solutions, our comprehensive understanding of the functional problem using PrecisionPS creates direct insight into the precise functional solution. By establishing conflict-free conditions for collaborative problem solving, we create collective ownership of the functional solution with an inspired commitment to developing and implementing our functional plan. The precision of the functional solution empowers us to effectively and efficiently implement our functional plan using PDSA and achieve sustained transformative results.

PrecisionPS is a comprehensive transformation paradigm that cannot be applied in fragments. Most of us are unaware of our innate conflict-solving mindset, and beginning with "Learning to Look," our subsequent PrecisionPS steps advance and reinforce our ability to problem solve together. Compassionate facilitation is the critical catalyst that empowers teams to move from conflict to collaborative problem solving by connecting the PrecisionPS principles to our power tools, and this is worth considering as a separate question.

Precision Problem Solving: Look, Understand, Act

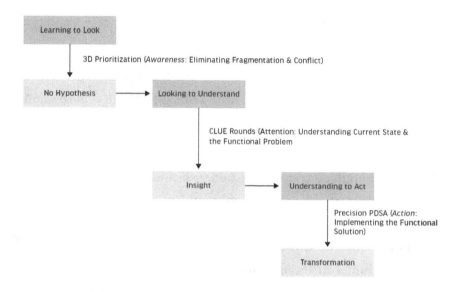

Learning to Look

3D Prioritization (*Awareness*: Eliminating Fragmentation & Conflict)

No Hypothesis → Looking to Understand

CLUE Rounds (Attention: Understanding Current State & the Functional Problem

Insight → Understanding to Act

Precision PDSA (*Action*: Implementing the Functional Solution)

Transformation

3. Compassionate Facilitation Is a Critical Part of PrecisionPS. Can You Expand on the Function of Being a Facilitator and Doing Facilitation?

Facilitation means "to make easy, to simplify," and our role as facilitators is a synergistic combination of *being* and *doing*. A core objective with our use of PrecisionPS is to arrive at a shared understanding of the functional problem, *what actually is*, which intuitively reveals the functional solution. In contrast to the conventional consulting approach of implementing preconceived solutions, our function as PrecisionPS facilitators is to guide and support teams with an approach to developing and implementing a functional plan of their own by:

- becoming aware of and understanding the nature of conflict (Learning to Look),

- seeing and understanding our current state of activity and the functional problem (Looking to Understand), and

- having a collective insight into the functional solution and developing and implementing a functional plan (Understanding to Act).

Understanding the nature of conflict and "Learning to Look" are the critical foundations to compassionate facilitation and PrecisionPS.

As facilitators, we can only offer guidance and support in areas we understand, which means that we must first understand the nature of conflict ourselves. Understanding begins with awareness of how we constantly buffet in the fragmented turbulence of *what we think is* and *what we think should be.* To look at our sources of fragmentation, such as our values, traditions, knowledge, and experience, we must be vulnerable, letting go of our defenses, looking deeply within, and exposing ourselves to potential emotional distress. In letting go of our defenses, our sensitivity is heightened, and we begin to perceive our inner and outer surroundings with authenticity, looking objectively at our fragmentation and the conflicts we create. The combination of being aware, vulnerable, sensitive, and authentic creates conditions for understanding the nature of conflict.

There is no doing, no how, no gradual progression to authenticity. You are authentic, or you are not. Authenticity cannot be feigned; we are very sensitive to disingenuous displays.

THE STORY OF THREE APOLOGIES

The spouse of a hospital trustee was admitted to the hospital with appendicitis for an appendectomy. She had a history of developing blood clots and needed to resume her blood-thinning medication after the surgery. For unclear reasons, the patient did not receive her medication until the following day. The medication error triggered a cascade of bedside apologies. The surgeon apologized first on behalf of the nurses caring for her, blaming them for not having contacted him to write the medication order. The hospital risk manager then came by and offered a scripted apology that upheld the hospital's commitment to patient safety and deflected responsibility to the surgeon. Finally, the hospital CEO stopped by and offered a heartfelt apology, assuming full responsibility for the error and assuring the patient that there would be a full investigation with corrective action. Fortunately, the patient didn't experience any complications and was discharged home. In a follow-up conversation between the trustee and the hospital CEO, the trustee shared that of the three apologies his wife had received, the only meaningful apology for her was the one the CEO had offered. He was authentic.

Our understanding of the nature of conflict releases us from its grasp, enabling us to authentically engage teams with open-mindedness, attentive listening, and compassion. This is a state of *being* rather than *doing*. Being compassionate facilitators enables us to create a safe learning environment for teams, which empowers team members to share openly and collaborate. This is the foundation for problem solving together.

In addition to creating conditions for a safe, collaborative learning environment, compassionate facilitation also creates the broader capacity for open observation and inquiry; our freedom to look without assumption, judgment, or hypothesis removes our subjective constraints and empowers us to objectively see and understand *what actually is* and clarify the functional problem. These attributes are our innate state of being, and we interconnect our PrecisionPS principles and tools with compassionate facilitation to understand, develop, and implement transformative solutions to functional problems. Thus, we must also have technical training and expertise in operating the tools. We must understand the systems, participatory management, and peer support principles that synergistically power PrecisionPS, and we have to understand how to skillfully use 3D Prioritization, CLUE Rounds, and PDSA as PrecisionPS power tools. The synergistic integration of *being* and *doing* positions us as PrecisionPS catalysts; our function is to simplify and accelerate our capability for problem solving together without being part of the outcome. In other words, as compassionate facilitators, we empower teams to collaboratively tap their collective genius to understand and solve functional problems. The functional solution is the team's collaborative creation.

Every team member begins with fragmented perceptions, each thinking they know *what is* and *what should be*, and our capacity for understanding conflict is variable, requiring our continued attention throughout the PrecisionPS progression. Change is intimately related to conflict. The more personal the change, the greater the conflict and resistance to change, and it is much easier to make incremental changes in the margins than to be fundamentally transformed. For example, it's much easier for us to make food shopping adjustments to accommodate a family member's new diagnosis of diabetes than it is to be the diabetic family member who has to change their diet and behavior. By integrating our understanding of conflict (*being*) with our expertise in applying PrecisionPS principles and tools (*doing*), compassionate facilitation provides us with the best opportunity for transformative rather than incremental change. Our *being* compassionate facilitators is always integrated with our *doing* functional facilitation, and if we separate the two, conflict and suboptimal results are inevitable.

4. Can You Clarify the Distinction between Ideas and Insight-Generated Solutions?

We live in a world replete with fragmented and contradictory ideas, a blend of objective facts and subjective ideas, which we have a hard time discerning. Let's start with some definitions. A fact is "that which is *actually* happening, a thing that is proved to be true," whereas an idea is "a thought as to a possible course of action, a concept, a hypothesis." We like to think that we are objective problem solvers and that our ideas enable factual improvement, but we have a strong subjective element to our ideas that dominates. We have popular quotes that underscore the power of subjective thought, such as:

- "Emotion trumps logic every time." —Campbell MacPherson

- "Culture eats strategy for breakfast." —Peter Drucker

As we have seen before, we create conflict when we create subjective divisions like culture and strategy or emotion and logic. The same thing happens when we fragment our reality with facts and ideas.

Ideas are an output of thought, and to understand the nature of ideas, we must understand the nature of thought. We have seen how we subjectively interpret our surroundings and functional problems with our values, traditions, education, and experiences, which divide and contradict. Our subjective mental models limit and distort our perceptions, preventing us from seeing what *actually is*, and our lack of understanding forms the basis for what *we think is* and what *we think should be*. This is the core fragmentation-conflict cycle, and we can see how our ideas are generated to "conflict solve" as opinions, concepts, and hypotheses; we fill in our lack of understanding with ideas, which generates subjective knowledge and solutions by abstraction.

THE STORY OF EXTREMES (PART ONE)

I like cycling and always challenge myself to extremes in everything that I do. I have an image of professional cyclists in the Tour de France, and although I know that I will never come anywhere close to being that competitive, I nevertheless benchmark my personal cycling targets in alignment with them. I buy an expensive lightweight graphite racing bike and begin an intense training routine, riding long distances and prioritizing hill climbs. My middle-age physique is not capable of maintaining the training rigor, and in very short order, I begin to develop muscle strain and joint pain in my legs. I rationalize that the pain is more a test of my mental fortitude than a harbinger of injury and resolve to continue training. No pain, no gain. I press on and develop severe patellar tendonitis, or "biker's knee," and have to stop training completely. "It's just a flesh wound," I say to myself. "I'll be back at it in no time."

Is there anything new in ideas? In addition to being fragmented and incomplete, our accumulated knowledge is retrospective, historical no matter how recent, and stored as memory in our brains, books, databases, and on the internet. So, ideas that we like to think of as new and innovative are a repackaging and reconfiguring of what we already know, subjective and objective. When we see that generating ideas is our best attempt to solve problems with our limited knowledge, we understand that our solutions can never be complete; our outcomes will at best be iterative partial improvements in the form of more, better, and different:

- More of the same (train harder and faster)

- The same thing better (develop a better training routine)

- The same thing different (buy a high-end racing bike)

Our propensity to live in abstraction circumvents us from making the time and effort to understand *what actually is*, and we jump to solutions. We think we know *what should be* based on the ideas and images we have generated from our interpretation of *what is*. In an environment where crises abound, we become problem-solving firefighters, quickly extinguishing visible flames while leaving the white-hot embers untouched beneath the smoke and ashes. The problems flare again, and before we know it, we're putting out the same fires with new ones. We enable wildfire conditions rather than making things better. In all the urgency and confusion, we don't have the time or capacity to do much beyond reactive firefighting, and this becomes our established approach to quality, safety, and performance improvement. Our complex and clouded environment doesn't allow us to see what the functional problem *actually is*.

If our thought-derived ideas can't provide us with new, functional, and sustained solutions, what can? Our ideas are outputs of subjective interpretation, reconfigurations, and enhancements to our limited knowledge and understanding. To let go of ideas, we have to Learn to Look to understand how we interpret what we perceive and contradict ourselves.

In Learning to Look, we can observe openly, without assumptions, interpretations, or ideas; we inquire with no hypothesis. Now, we're in business. Open or impartial observation with no hypothesis empowers us to clearly see and understand the current state and the functional problem. Our comprehensive understanding of the functional problem creates the space for insight into the functional solution.

THE STORY OF EXTREMES (PART TWO)

Being unable to cycle while I recover from my biker's knee injury, I have time to look at my exercise training regimen without distraction. I become aware that, as much as I enjoy cycling, I really dislike the stress and fatigue I self-impose with my extreme objectives. In a twisted way, I'm actually happy that I can't ride my bike.

I explore why I feel compelled to associate exercise with competitive training and see that I have all kinds of embedded assumptions and expectations that drive my approach. I want to stand out as an athlete among my friends and colleagues, and to do that, I need to achieve exceptional performance milestones. I also see that my body has its own intelligence that I'm ignoring or overruling with my desires. I'm not listening to the messages it continuously provides about the physical and emotional harm I'm inflicting. In seeing all this, I understand that I'm constantly in conflict as I attempt to reconcile my contradictory desires and objectives and that my mental models about what I think is happening generate my ideas about exercise and *what I think should be.* I have an insight that there is no need or value in pursuing objectives that set me up for physical injury and emotional conflict, and that I can easily create a cycling routine that is healthy and enjoyable. By letting go of my expectations and being attentive to my physical and emotional state, I can continuously adjust my activities with effortless alignment.

We have to be very careful when describing insight. In contrast to ideas, insight is not a knowledge-based reflection of thought. Since we innately use subjective thought to shape our perspectives, we are susceptible to turning insight into an idea, into an action that *we should do.* We need to remember that the description is not the described; it's not what you're thinking. Insight is "the capacity to gain an accurate and deep intuitive understanding, a perception that is unerring, direct, and immediate."

Insight is like a light suddenly switched on in a dark room, providing a clear, integrated understanding of the functional problem and solution. There is no how to insight. We can't make it happen, and anything we do to make it happen ensures that it won't. The opening for having insight comes when we observe without hypothesis and let go of our personal motivations and attachments to desired outcomes. When there's nothing specifically in it for us, the functional solution applies to everyone as correct action.

The actions of insight and ideas are distinct. In contrast to our ideas, which generate reactive and proactive responses, insight creates immediate action. That is, while our ideas are always time-bound concepts, linking our accumulated knowledge to our present and future state, *what we think is* and *what we think should be*, insight arises from our direct observation of *what actually is* and always acts in the moment. We use iterative improvement to implement idea-generated plans, subjectively and objectively modifying our activities to achieve successively closer approximations to our ideal solution, *what we think should be*. In distinction, we use continuous improvement to implement insight-created plans, making continual objective and synergistic changes with our hypothesis-free observation of *what actually is*.

THE STORY OF EXTREMES (PART THREE)

My knee injury is healed, and I can begin cycling again. My approach is transformed with my insight. I have no predetermined objectives other than to cycle for the exercise and to be mindful of my physical and mental well-being. I pay attention to the feedback I receive from my body. I learn to distinguish signs of physical fatigue from signs of strain. I learn to listen to support my body's need for hydration and sustenance during longer rides. I learn to call it a day when my body says, "Enough." I also learn to ride just to get out and take in the scenery. My joy for cycling reawakens, and I find that my strength and endurance are increasing well beyond what I thought possible during my crazed competitive days. But none of that matters; I'm just harmoniously riding my bike.

Consider all the hype and effort going into developing and implementing artificial intelligence (AI). Based on our understanding of the nature of thought, ideas, and insight, where does AI sit? AI programming, algorithms, and training data sets are all based on our inputs, using our accumulated subjective and objective knowledge. AI is already demonstrating accelerated thought-like capabilities through its ability to rapidly access vast repositories of data and information, and, like human thought, it is also exposing its inability to discern facts and ideas.

Since our accumulated knowledge, no matter how vast, is always fragmented and incomplete, AI won't ever provide us with comprehensive understanding of functional problems or solutions any more than our innate thought processes will. We are using our material thought process to build AI in our own image. Comprehensive understanding and insight reside outside of thought, meaning they will also remain outside of AI. Like thought, AI will reconfigure what we know but will not create anything new. Hopefully, AI developers will understand this limitation and focus their attention on developing and refining AI capabilities that discern objective from subjective knowledge. With distinct objective AI capability correctly positioned to support our understanding of *what actually is*, our insight-created functional solutions and plans may have enhanced opportunity for sustained success.

When Opportunity Knocks, Take It or Leave It

What I like best about flying is the freedom it affords to navigate an ocean of air and see the earth from a wider perspective. I never tire of the beauty of the earth by day or the sky by night.

—CHESLEY "SULLY" SULLENBERGER

I have always wanted to be a pilot, and there were instances throughout my medical training when aviation would surface as a wishful alternative. I was on a hardcore surgeon track as a medical student, and while I was far into the process of applying for ENT residencies, I discovered that there were residencies in aviation medicine; I hadn't ever considered any aviation-related medical specialty, and at this point, it was too late.

I also had low points during residency training, where I lamented not being in aviation and had fleeting thoughts of doing something in the field other than being a pilot, like becoming an air traffic controller or a flight attendant. All this to say that my wife at the time saw my continued passion for aviation, and on Father's Day, the month I finished my anesthesia fellowship in 1997, she gave me a gift certificate for an introductory flight lesson. I was stunned, incredibly excited on one hand and deeply apprehensive on the other. A door that I had barricaded shut for fear of failure had been unlocked for me with a red-carpet invitation to walk through.

Here I was with my opportunity to take on one of my deepest desires and conflicts, and perhaps I was in a different mindset after my prior pivotal career moments where I had to make sudden reactive adjustments to progress. Like my option to switch from ENT to anesthesia, this was a moment where I felt I had to either move ahead or permanently drop the ambition.

Unlike the specialty pivot, however, where I had to initiate an action plan for the anesthesia resident's proposition that "it was never too late to change," my invitation to fly was being handed to me on a platter. All I had to do was take it or leave it. Despite the barriers I had put up all these years to protect the dream, I knew this was my best opportunity, and I had to go for it. It was time to let go of my fears and see what would happen. With excitement and some undeniable trepidation, I thanked my wife, saying, "You have no idea what you've just done. If this works out, I'm going for my pilot's license!"

THE MOMENT OF TRUTH

My introductory flight lesson had no physical exam requirements, and as my flight instructor guided me with my first takeoff in our Cessna 152, I was bursting with joy. All my pent-up emotions and aspirations for this moment were released. Even if this turned out to be the only opportunity to pilot, I had broken through my inner sound barrier and was game to take this forward as far as it would go. I declared my commitment to train and was assigned a newly hired flight instructor for my weekly lessons.

My flight lessons were the highlight of my week, and I eagerly absorbed all the training as I prepared for my first solo flight. My flight instructor hadn't explicitly requested documentation for my flight physical during this first phase of pre-solo training, and I just rolled with it, waiting for that moment of reckoning. I successfully completed my first solo flight, and it wasn't until I landed, elated with my accomplishment, that my flight instructor sheepishly informed me that I should have had a documented flight physical before the solo. Oops. To continue, I would need to get the flight physical done. So, there I was, at my dreaded moment of truth.

I hadn't experienced anything during my flight training thus far that even remotely suggested my color deficit was impacting my ability to fly safely. I was confident that I was not being reckless in my pilot pursuit. At the same time, I still had the same assumptions that Federal Aviation Administration (FAA) regulations would prevent me from getting my pilot's license. I was resigned with what seemed like an inevitable end to my training. It was what it was, and I had nothing to lose, so I made an appointment with a flight surgeon, ready to accept whatever came out of it.

STRIKE ONE—THE FLIGHT PHYSICAL

My flight physical went as expected. I was in good health with no remarkable findings until I took the color plate vision test, which consisted of a series of circles containing color-shaded dots forming numbers that people with normal vision could see. I failed. My results confirmed that I had a red-green color deficit. I was deflated but not surprised, almost relieved to have this self-imposed drama finally over with.

Yet, as the flight surgeon reviewed my color test with me, to my great surprise, he affirmed that full color vision was not an absolute requisite for safe, competent flying, and that there was a practical color test that could be administered to assess essential color vision for aviation. If I passed that exam, I would be eligible for a Statement of Demonstrated Ability, a SODA, which would serve as my flight physical clearance for satisfactory color vision. I would have to request an examination with an FAA inspector, who would conduct the test at the airport. A gate that I didn't know about had suddenly opened. Perhaps this wasn't over just yet!

STRIKE TWO—LIGHT GUN TEST #1

I made my appointment and showed up a few weeks later at the airport for my color test with the FAA inspector. He was a hard-core, by-the-book administrator who immediately shared his negative feelings about certifying pilots with vision deficits. I was in trouble.

The inspector informed me that I would be taking a light gun color test, where an air traffic controller in the control tower would flash a random sequence of white, green, and red lights at me. My instructions were to identify and call out the colors as they were flashed my way.

If I incorrectly identified any flash, the test would be over, and I would fail. I faced the tower with full concentration as the controller proceeded to rapidly fire flash color sequences at me so quickly that I could not keep up with the naming after each flash. I realized the test was not passable for anybody, and I stopped and looked at the inspector in disbelief. He radioed the controller to stop and curtly said, "You failed."

I felt dejected and irritated by the test approach and the outcome. As I waited at the front desk for the FAA inspector to complete the documentation, the receptionist stepped up to me and, in a low voice, shared that my inspector failed everyone and that I could take the light gun test again if I reapplied. She suggested finding a date when a different inspector was on and taking the test on an overcast day when the light gun signals were most visible. Once again, another portal had opened by being present, aware, and letting things unfold. The goal of flying was still alive!

THE HIT—LIGHT GUN TEST #2

Two weeks later, I was back at the airport, this time with another FAA inspector, whose approach was in complete juxtaposition to the first one. This inspector was committed to having me pass and explained that the light gun test was intended to ensure that a pilot could receive tower communication via colored light signals for safe landings in the setting of radio failure.

Prior to taking the test, he suggested that we do a couple of practice sequences so I could familiarize myself with the test. Wow, what a difference. We stood on the tarmac facing the control tower to begin the practice session. Once again, the inspector reassured me that it was OK if I got the colors wrong during practice. The controller flashed three times on the inspector's signal, and I rattled off, "Red, green, white." My quick response seemed to startle the inspector, who looked at me pleased and said, "You got them all correct, so we're done. You pass!"

Passing the test was an incredible moment. I was in the clear to get my private pilot's license with no restrictions. I received my SODA documentation, resumed my training, and obtained my private pilot's license six months later.

WE ARE OUR BIGGEST BARRIER; KEEP ON LOOKING

With my private pilot's license in hand, I looked back over the twenty-year interval between my high school dream of becoming a pilot and finally being cleared for takeoff, wondering how different my life might have been had I taken the leap at the beginning. I might have become a commercial pilot. I might have chosen a medical specialty that enabled me to incorporate flying. Or perhaps nothing would have changed. I had no regrets on how this had played out. By the time I had completed my private pilot training, I had a family, was a board-certified anesthesiologist, and was well into my second semester of business school.

The point of this piloting follow-up is not to dwell on past speculation but rather to highlight the impact that conflict, *what we think is* and *what we think should be,* has on our lives. The intensity of our conflict and emotional resistance to change skyrockets the more our deep-seated assumptions and desires are threatened. I had hardwired a collection of dissuading self-imposed assumptions and outside opinions about my visual color deficit as an impossible barrier to flying, which was in extreme contradiction with my dream of becoming a pilot.

I was afraid of confronting what I assumed would be a definitive "no" to my dream, so I shut down all avenues of objectively looking at my "impossible" problem. Instead, I imposed a separate set of brash assumptions to doggedly pursue alternate career opportunities that I insisted were possible and correct, learning the hard way through pivotal failures that looking at problems openly, without expectations, always revealed incredible options.

Our emotions trump logic every time. I couldn't see the rationale of looking openly at my impenetrable flying conflict until I received the gift certificate for my first flight lesson. That packaged invitation to fly was my emotional release from the no-fly-zone that had restricted me from looking, understanding, and acting for so long. The opportunity was in front of me, and I just had to say yes and show up. Everything that followed—flying solo, getting my SODA, and ultimately obtaining my pilot's license—came from continuous observation, letting go of assumptions, and acting on opportunities as they emerged. What I thought was impossible became possible.

When we see and understand how our subjective assumptions, limited knowledge, and desires create conflict and fear-driven responses, we can move beyond our confusion to objectively observe and attend to *what actually is.* We are our biggest barrier to functional problem solving, and our greatest opportunity is Learning to Look, to observe openly, at ourselves, each other, and the systems we live in, with no hypothesis. When we are free to look, the rest follows naturally: compassionate problem solving together, Looking to Understand our functional problems, and Understanding to Act with insight on functional solutions. It's not what you're thinking. Keep on looking.